Urbanization, Population Growth, and Economic Development in the Philippines

STUDIES IN POPULATION AND URBAN DEMOGRAPHY
SERIES EDITOR: KINGSLEY DAVIS

Changing Sex Differential in Morality
Robert D. Retherford

Teenage Marriages: A Demographic Analysis
John R. Weeks

URBANIZATION, POPULATION GROWTH, AND ECONOMIC DEVELOPMENT IN THE PHILIPPINES

Ernesto del Mar Pernia

International Population and Urban Research
University of California, Berkeley

**Studies in Population and
Urban Demography, Number 3**

GREENWOOD PRESS
WESTPORT, CONNECTICUT • LONDON, ENGLAND

β. 1850

Library of Congress Cataloging in Publication Data

Pernia, Ernesto M   1943-
    Urbanization, population growth, and economic development
in the Philippines.

    (Studies in population and urban demography; no. 3)
    Bibliography: p.
    Includes index.
    1. Urbanization—Philippine Islands. 2. Philippine
Islands—Economic conditions—1946-   3. Philippine Islands—
Population. 4. Migration, Internal—Philippine Islands. I. Title.
II. Series.
HT147.P6P472   330.9'599'04   77-24588
ISBN 0-8371-9721-X

Library of Congress Catalog Card Number: 77-24588
ISBN: 0-8371-9721-X
ISSN: 0147-1104

First published in 1977

Greenwood Press, Inc.
51 Riverside Avenue, Westport, Connecticut 06880

Printed in the United States of America

CONTENTS

TABLES

FIGURES AND MAPS

ACKNOWLEDGMENTS

My indebtedness to several persons who helped in the preparation of this work is immeasurable.

Dr. Kingsley Davis introduced me to the intriguing field of urbanization and economic development and encouraged me to pursue the Philippine case as a topic for research. He helped me clarify and develop my seminal thinking on the subject. He continued to be a source of inspiration even when I was in the field collecting data, analyzing them, and writing up the drafts. And he eased the pains of revising the drafts with his able and untiring guidance. Dr. Michael L. Wiseman was generous with his time in providing criticisms, especially on the econometric portion of the study. Dr. Robert R. Reed helped me improve the analysis of historical data by applying some qualitative flavor to the mass of quantitative data.

I am deeply grateful to Dr. Mercedes B. Concepción, Dean of the Population Institute, University of the Philippines, for affording me the opportunity to work on my research at the Institute. In addition to completing my research, I benefited greatly from my close association with her and from my experience as Visiting Lecturer and Research Associate at the Institute. Funds during my stay at the Institute were provided by the Smithsonian Institution's Interdisciplinary Communications Program.

Two former colleagues at the Population Institute deserve to be mentioned. Dr. Peter C. Smith gave constructive comments on earlier drafts of certain chapters, pointed out relevant materials to me, and aided me in using them. Dr. Gerry E. Hendershot was always willing to discuss my ideas and problems.

I wish to thank the staff of the Population Institute for a variety of ancillary services. Nellie Mangubat extended programming assistance, and Judith Subido, Lucretia Maria Singson, and Solita Soriano provided research assistance. Erlinda Atendido, Rita Gunable, and Felicitas Nebres all helped type earlier drafts. Emerenciana Prospero typed the final draft. I also thank Ann C. Mine of IPUR for able editorial assistance and Gregory Chu of East-West Population Institute for the nice cartographic work.

Finally, I cannot fail to mention my wife, Elena, for her understanding and moral support. To her and to our child, Patricia, I dedicate this book.

Ernesto M. Pernia
School of Economics
University of the Philippines

March 1977

Urbanization, Population Growth, and Economic Development in the Philippines

INTRODUCTION 1

BACKGROUND

The spatial distribution of population is an aspect of demographic change that until recently, has attracted relatively little concern. "Population problems" have popularly connoted population growth or decline via the more discernible phenomena of fertility and mortality. The distribution of people at a point in time or over space and time is more difficult to discern. For one thing, the processes of urbanization and migration are slow and subtle. Moreover, it is more difficult to measure and to collect data on these processes than on fertility and mortality. And, too, urbanization and migration are less dramatic.

Increasingly, however, it has been realized that the distributional aspects of population deserve as much attention as, if not more than, the traditional population concerns. While there remains some disagreement as to whether or not the size and growth of population are excessive, there seems to be near consensus with respect to its spatial imbalance. While we know that by the year 2000 the Philippine population would more or less double to about 80 million, we have at best a vague inkling of its rural/urban/metropolitan distribution at the national, regional, and provincial levels. While we know that birth and death rates would probably fall by some amount, we can only guess as to whence and whither people will be moving or for what reasons. Thus, the size and composition of the population may be a less important problem than the pace and extent of urbanization, the directions migration will take, and the factors that will influence these processes.

There is now a growing social concern for a long-term perspective on development policy and planning. This concern emanates from the awareness that, while not much can be done in terms of altering present structures and patterns of population, environment, and income, several changes are yet feasible for the next generation.[1] But planning for the future cannot be sensibly executed without a balanced awareness of past trends, patterns, and relationships. While a retrospective understanding may not suffice, it is important because possible future deviations from the trend can be better appreciated and handled. Urbanization is a significant aspect of population distribution that needs to be carefully examined so that an intelligent grasp of it can be incorporated in a national development policy for the future.[2] The present study may be considered a pioneering attempt in that direction. It aims to investigate urbanization and rural-urban migration as they relate to socioeconomic development in the Philippines.

The principal questions that serve to guide the study are the following: (1) what have been the pace and patterns of urbanization during the first seventy years of the twentieth century; (2) to what extent has rural-urban migration contributed to the growth of urban population; (3) what socioeconomic factors have accounted for the variations in levels and rates of urbanization among regions and provinces; (4) what have been the major migration streams and what has been the relative importance of rural-urban streams; and (5) how have the migrants in the different streams differed among themselves, and the migrants from the nonmigrants in terms of their demographic and socioeconomic characteristics?

RELATED PREVIOUS STUDIES

Previous research efforts have examined Philippine urbanization in various ways. A traditional concept of urbanization has been the growth or development of cities. Philippine cities and their development have been described by Cressey (1958 and 1960) and Spencer (1958). Fujimoto (1968) utilized scalogram analysis to delve into the complexity of towns and cities and to explain how these communities diversify as they mature. Ullman (1960) examined their functions especially as centers for both domestic and foreign trade. Mariano (1975) tried to relate in-migration to urban development in a number of cities and concluded that the in-migration rate rises as a city matures and then declines after reaching a certain saturation point.

Urban concentration or primacy has induced other scholars to view urbanization in terms of the singular growth of Metropolitan Manila and its associated opportunities and problems.[3] For example, Laquian (1966) stressed the key political and administrative role played by Manila in the development of the nation. Hollnsteiner (1969) looked into the evolution of Manila, providing an historical and anthropological perspective on its contemporary problems, and more recently (1974) tried to explain why urban planning as practiced has largely failed to solve those problems. Hendershot (1969) elaborated further on Metro Manila's problems. Thus, the frequent reference to the primate city has inevitably led to a concept of urbanization that is synonymous with its favorable or unfavorable growth.

Recent concern about dispersed development, however, has riveted research interest to urbanization covering regions or groups of regions. Smith (1970), for example, on the basis of principal-components analysis applied to municipal-level data, specified three major dimensions underlying urbanization and socioeconomic development in Lowland Luzon, to wit, SES, population buildup, and literacy. Abenoja (1975) attempted to delimit urban places in Central and Eastern Visayas and produced urbanization scores for the different municipalities that correlated closely with the proportion urban in those places. A similar exercise was carried out for Mindanao municipalities by Smith and Bouis (1975). Finally, Pascual (1972) provided an overview on national urbanization using data made available by the 1970 Census, but this work was brief and purely descriptive. Still needed are studies that analyze national and subnational urbanization trends, as well as rural-urban migration streams, and that relate them to population growth and socioeconomic development. The present study is meant, in part, to fill the gap.

CURRENT PUBLIC POLICY

Perhaps because the concern about population distribution is so recent, the government has not come up with an explicit policy on national urbanization and migration. Various measures to grapple with traffic, sewerage, slums, and pollution in Metro Manila approach what might be considered an urban policy. At the national level, there has been renewed concern for rural development, industrial dispersal, and regional development (Republic of the Philippines, 1973). However, these national policies, which obviously have a direct bearing on population distribution, do not expressly articulate their linkages with urbanization and migration.

National population policy is nevertheless designed to reduce the rate of population growth through the family planning program. The revised Population Act of 1971, Section 2, contains the following Declaration of Policy:

> The Government of the Philippines hereby declares that for the purpose of furthering the national development, increasing the share of each Filipino in the fruits of economic progress and meeting the grave social and economic challenge of high rate of population growth, a national program of family planning involving both public and private sectors which respect the religious beliefs and values of the individuals involved shall be undertaken (Presidential Decree No. 79, 1972).

For this reason, the Commission on Population (POPCOM) was created, among whose objectives (Section 4 of Revised Population Act of 1971) is "to propose policies and programs that will guide and regulate labor force participation, internal migration and spatial distribution of population consistent with national development." To date, however, the POPCOM has not pursued this particular objective by means of a well-defined program. It is now concerned with the "new thrust" of the National Population Program described by the executive director as follows:

> The need to respond to these problems (the shift to less effective contraceptive methods, the increasing number of dropouts, and the plateauing of acceptor's rate) and the necessity of bringing the program closer to the people has brought about the development of the new thrust of the program, the *Total Integrated Development Approach.* This new orientation seeks to shift the approach from what had been dominantly a contraceptive-oriented program to a concept-oriented program. This is based on the firm belief that when the program becomes conceptually understood and accepted as a way of life worth living,

the people will seek on their own—in accordance with their moral
and religious convictions—the services they can continuously
avail of, except abortion. (Esmundo, 1975:3).

THEORETICAL FRAMEWORK

A popular assertion regarding urbanization in contemporary developing countries is that it has been proceeding at a rapid pace (e.g., UNESCO,
1957; Terzo, 1972). This development is considered to be a consequence
of the acceleration in population growth during the past two and a half
decades. Accordingly, a high rate of population growth has provoked massive internal population movements, particularly migrations from rural
to urban areas. Rural-to-urban flows have supposedly been impelled by
conditions of high density, unemployment, and poverty in rural areas.
However, since urban areas are already overcrowded, such migration merely
aggravates the deteriorating conditions in these areas (e.g., McGee, 1971;
Myrdal, 1968). The conclusion is therefore inescapable. Rapid urbanization, merely an outcome of rapid population growth, has been related
minimally, if at all, to development (Weitz, 1973). Many believe it might
even have hampered the development process, and hence should be curbed.

To what extent is the impression of rapid urbanization and its lack of
linkage to development true in the case of the Philippines? This study
argues that this impression is largely a false one emanating from a confused
concept of urbanization.[4] As we have pointed out above, past research
has unqualifiedly used the term *urbanization* to refer to the growth of
cities, particularly the primate city. This practice has tended to dichoto-
mize Philippine society into the "Manileños" (those who reside in Manila
and its suburbs) and the "provincianos" (those who belong to all other
areas of the country). Thus, rural-to-urban migration has come to mean
(almost exclusively) residential transfer from the "provincia" to Manila.
A migrant in Manila is invariably dubbed a "provinciano" (rural-urban
migrant), and one who goes elsewhere is said to be moving to the "provincia" (urban-rural migrant). It may be noted that this perception has been
the common one, even though the move is between a secondary city
(like Cebu, Bacolod, or Davao) and Manila. In this way, the phenomenal
expansion of Manila may have been construed as rapid urbanization in
the Philippines.

In this study, we depart from the traditional and popular concept of urbanization and adopt that concept which inheres in the term itself. We conceive of urbanization as the transformation of society from rural to urban. Hence, intrinsic in this concept are two related conditions: (1) that the transformation process involves the whole population, not just those in the country's central city or metropolitan area; and (2) that the growth of urban population is considered not in absolute terms but relative to the rural population. Viewed in these terms, urbanization can be related to population growth and development in a manner that may be counter to the common supposition.

We propose that urbanization is influenced negatively by population growth and positively by socioeconomic development. Schematically, the relationships may be depicted in a simplified framework as follows:

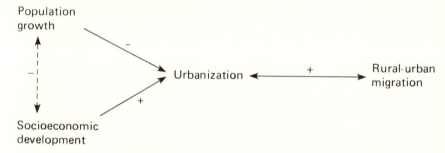

The negative effect of population growth or higher fertility on urbanization can come about in three ways: (1) directly, because an acceleration in population growth is normally greater in the rural sector than in the urban sector; (2) directly, because high fertility entails a greater dependency burden which tends to retard mobility; and (3) indirectly, through its negative consequence on socioeconomic development. On the other hand, development can affect urbanization in three positive ways: (1) directly, because rural development in terms of higher agricultural productivity, higher literacy, and communication levels tends to occasion greater rural-urban migration; (2) directly, because urban development in the way of jobs and other human commodities attracts in-migrants; and (3) indirectly, through its negative effect on population growth. In addition, we hypothesize a two-way positive relationship between urbanization and rural-urban migration. On the one hand, rural-urban migration may be viewed as itself a component of urbanization. On the other hand, more urbanized regions or urban areas tend to attract migrants not only in terms of volume but also in terms of positive selections. Moreover, rural-urban interchange migration is expected to increase as the country advances in urbanization.

OPERATIONAL CONCEPTS AND DEFINITIONS

Several definitions of urbanization have been advanced. A classic definition is that of Eldridge (1942:311) who considers urbanization to be "a process of population concentration. It proceeds in two ways: the multiplication of points of concentration and the increase in the size of individual concentrations." According to Davis (1965:3-4), "it refers to the proportion of the total population concentrated in urban settlements, or else to a rise in this proportion." Both definitions subsume the notion of concentration. But Eldridge seems to refer more to the growth of urban population (absolute "urbanization"), while Davis is concerned with such growth relative to the growth of rural population (relative urbanization). Although urban growth and urbanization are inseparable, they are sufficiently distinct and the distinction should be stressed here. For, while urbanization hinges on the growth of both urban and rural populations, urban growth as such is independent of rural population growth. For instance, urban population may be growing fast, but because rural population is also increasing at nearly the same rate, urbanization will be slow.[5] The distinction between urbanization and urban growth is analogous to that between economic development and economic growth—economic development referring to structural and qualitative changes and economic growth to gross increases in national product (Kindleberger, 1958:3).[6]

The definition of urbanization we prefer to adopt here connotes the transformation of population, as mentioned above. It takes into account not only the urban population but also the rural population which, in a developing country, is the much larger component of total population. Accordingly, we use the following basic working definitions: the *level* or *degree* of urbanization is the proportion (percentage) of the population living in urban places; *urbanization* as such (or the process of) means the rise in the urban proportion; the *rate of urban growth* is the percentage change in urban population during an interval (and similarly for rate of rural growth); the *tempo* or *pace* of urbanization is the difference between the urban and the rural rates of growth;[7] and *primacy* is the ratio of the population of the largest city to the combined populations of the next three largest cities. Another simple measure of urban primacy is the share of urban or total population concentrated in the country's largest city or metropolitan area. Both indices are meant to reflect the general pattern whereby urbanization has been proceeding at the national level. A high primacy index, for example, would indicate that urbanization or urban growth is centralized, polarized, or unbalanced.

DATA AND METHODS

As in other less developed countries, it is difficult to draw an accurate picture of urbanization in the Philippines because of inadequate data. For one thing, past censuses did not make a count of urban population as distinct from rural population. For another, the urban criteria developed by the National Census and Statistics Office (NCSO, formerly Bureau of Census and Statistics) in 1963 are based on population size and density.[8] Although population size and density correlate closely with urban characteristics, no doubt some places are misclassified by said criteria. In other words, a place that ought to be considered urban by virtue of its social and economic institutions may be considered rural just because its population size or density falls short of the "urban minimum"; conversely, a place that possesses rural characteristics may be judged urban simply for meeting the size or density criterion.

For the 1970 Census, the NCSO (1973:6-8) developed a seemingly more precise definition of urban which, in addition to population size and density, takes into account certain urban institutional features, such as street patterns, commercial establishments, and economic and social activities. However plausible in itself, the 1970 urban definition has a drawback because it cannot be applied retrospectively to the past censuses, which do not contain urban institutional records. A worthwhile alternative is to apply the 1963 urban definition to all twentieth-century censuses (1903, 1918, 1939, 1948, 1960, and 1970) in order to derive consistent estimates of urbanization levels and trends. This procedure entails inspecting each municipality, *poblacion,* and *barrio* with their boundaries at each census date, and then culling urban inhabitants according to the urban criteria.[9]

Put succinctly, the 1963 urban definition[10] includes the following:

(1)   A whole municipality with a density of at least 1,000 per square kilometer.

(2)   In a municipality with a density of at least 500 per square kilometer:
   (a)   the *poblacion* of whatever size,
   (b)   a *barrio* of at least 2,500 population, and
   (c)   a *barrio* of at least 1,000 population and which is contiguous to the *poblacion.*

(3)   In a municipality of at least 20,000 population:
   (a)   the *poblacion* of whatever size, and
   (b)   a *barrio* of at least 2,500 population and which is contiguous to the *poblacion.*

(4)   A *poblacion* of at least 2,500 population.

An application of the 1963 and 1970 urban definitions to the 1970 Census reveals only slightly divergent results at the national and regional levels; at the provincial level, the differences are more noticeable (NCSO, 1973). We may assume that the results would be similar for the earlier censuses, i.e., the discrepancies would be negligible at the higher levels but would show up at the lower levels (provinces and municipalities). On balance, for the purpose of analyzing aggregate trends and patterns, the size-density definition may be as suitable as the one that includes institutional criteria. We can even argue that, although the 1970 definition is conceptually more plausible, the 1963 definition may offer more precise estimates because it is simpler to apply in practice. In fact, our test shows that provincial urbanization levels according to the 1963 definition correlate better with other socioeconomic indices (e.g., manufacturing and commercial establishments, radio ownership, literacy) than do urbanization levels according to the 1970 definition.

Apart from the various censuses on population, we also rely on agricultural and economic censuses for data on socioeconomic factors related to urbanization. For statistics on internal migration patterns, we tap the 1960 Census information on place of birth and current residence as well as the 1970 Census on place of residence in 1960 and current residence. The 1960 migration data are based on a 0.5 percent systematic sample, and the 1970 data on a 5.0 percent systematic sample of all households. For rural-urban migration patterns and their characteristics, we resort to the 1973 National Demographic Survey (NDS). The NDS was conducted in May 1973 by the University of the Philippine Population Institute (UPPI) in collaboration with the NCSO. It involved a nationwide representative sample of 8,434 households containing 52,760 persons.[11]

For the purposes of the present study, we exploit NDS Part II, Records 2 and 3, from which we created a special Record 4. This particular portion of the NDS deals with a sample of 28,482 persons aged fifteen or over who, when weighted (average weight = 790.4621), multiply to an estimated total of 22,513,942. Questions on place (and locale, whether rural or urban) of birth and residence at several points in time and on various demographic and socioeconomic characteristics were asked of these persons.

For a study such as this, a combination of different approaches and methods is necessary. To establish levels and tempos of urbanization over several decades, we have to utilize trend analysis of historical data that have been estimated, as described above, from raw census materials. To determine the relative speed of Philippine urbanization, this trend analysis must be used in conjunction with an analysis comparing Philippine data with those of other countries. To estimate the components of urban growth, we have first to determine places that were reclassified from rural to urban, and then to estimate rural-urban differential fertility and mortality (natural increase) from the 1973 NDS so that net rural-urban migration can be derived by the residual method. In order to assess the key determinants of urbanization, we have to make use of multiple regression analysis. Other approaches employed are those recommended by the United Nations (1970) Manual VI and (1974) Manual VIII for migration analysis, and standard cross-tabulation techniques.

ORGANIZATION OF THE STUDY

Following this introductory chapter are seven more chapters. Chapter 2 discusses the historical trends of urbanization and urban growth at the national and regional levels. In addition, it offers a comparative perspective on Philippine urbanization vis-à-vis a number of countries—those long developed, newly developed, and developing. In order to further assess the content of past urbanization, Chapter 3 provides an indirect procedure for estimating the sources or components of urban growth, discusses the results, and looks into the relative impacts of migration and natural increase on city growth. Chapter 4 examines the link of urbanization to development, first by comparing the Philippine experience with that of other Southeast and East Asian countries; then by analyzing the performance of the country's different regions; and, finally, by evaluating provincial data in a regression framework. Chapter 5 identifies the major internal migration streams in a framework that relates them to the regional development patterns. Chapter 6 attempts to analyze the characteristics of the different migration streams. Chapter 7 illustrates the prospects of urbanization and urban growth under different assumptions. Finally, Chapter 8 offers an overall summary, conclusions, and implications.

NOTES

1. Research programs that attempt to understand the possible courses of society to the year 2000 have been completed or are underway in both developed and developing countries, such as the United States, the United Kingdom, Australia, India, and South Korea. In the Philippines, a similar research program on "Population, Resources, Environment, and the Philippine Future" (PREPF) commenced in January 1975 and is scheduled to be completed by March 1977. It is being undertaken by the Development Academy of the Philippines, the School of Economics, and the Population Institute of the University of the Philippines.

2. The need for historical studies on urbanization and urban growth was indicated at a recent meeting of the International Union for the Scientific Study of Population (IUSSP) (Grebenik and Leridon, 1973:13). Urbanization is a major concern of the PREPF research program.

3. The notion of a primate city was first introduced by a geographer, Mark Jefferson (1939). For an elaborate treatment of the primate city in Southeast Asia, see Reed (1972).

4. In his study of world urbanization, Davis (1972) pointed out this illusion concerning less developed countries.

5. Davis (1965:5) puts it clearly: "A common mistake is to think of urbanization as simply the growth of cities. Since the total population is composed of both the urban population and the rural, however, the 'proportion urban' is a function of both of them. Accordingly cities can grow without any urbanization, provided that the rural population grows at an equal or a greater rate."

6. For example, a more meaningful indication of development is income distribution as reflected in the Gini ratio, or the proportion below some poverty threshold. Better income distribution can proceed quite independently of growth in GNP, and vice versa. For the Philippine experience, see Mangahas (1975).

7. An alternative measure is simply the percentage change in urbanization level or urban proportion during an interval, but this measure has inherent pitfalls. The United Nations (1974:26-31) Manual VIII recommends the urban-rural growth difference (URGD) as a superior measure.

8. The NCSO had earlier urban definitions in 1939 and 1948 but these were not applied, and the Philippine Statistical Survey of Household (PSSH) had another one in 1956. See NCSO (1973:2-4).

9. The NCSO (1973) did this exercise for 1948, 1960, and 1970 but not for the earlier censuses. We did it for all six censuses to ensure consistency. Our results for 1948, 1960, and 1970 are slightly different from those of the NCSO, even after we repeated the procedure.

10. Commentaries on this urban definition are found in the works of Bennett (1965) and Nazaret and Barretto (1963); a good discussion of its merits and demerits is provided by Smith (1970:141-152). Despite its shortcomings, the present author feels that it is sufficiently useful and meaningful.

11. The survey methodology is described in a series of documentation notes available at the UPPI. Also available are weighted marginals on all the records.

URBANIZATION TRENDS AND PATTERNS

2

One of the more significant features of populations in most countries is the degree to which they have become urban in recent years. In the Philippines, urbanization during the twentieth century has signified that one out of three Filipinos was living in an urban place in 1970 in contrast to only one in eight at the start of the century. In absolute numbers, the urban population increased from 1 million to 12 million during this period. If the trend continues to the year 2000, close to half of the population would become urbanites, numbering about 37 million or three times the magnitude in 1970. Urban places have grown not only in size but also in number. Thus, while in 1903 there were only 241 urban places, by 1970 these had mushroomed to more than 2,000, and cities multiplied from approximately five to sixty. At the same time, the number of towns or cities with 100,000 or more inhabitants increased from one to twenty-five.

This chapter focuses upon the trends and patterns of Philippine urbanization with a view to determining the speed and nature of the process. How did urbanization proceed during different historical periods of the present century at the national and regional levels? How did the postwar acceleration in population growth affect the pace of urbanization? How did urbanization in the Philippines compare with the historical experience of developed countries and the recent experience of countries in Asia? We proceed in this chapter by presenting a historical perspective, followed by a comparative analysis with developed and developing countries.

A HISTORICAL PERSPECTIVE, 1903-1970

The National Trends

The national level of urbanization in 1903 can be estimated at 13.1 percent.[1] This was similar to Sweden's level in 1870 and to that of Japan in 1887-1890 (Weber, 1899:110, 129). In other words, only about fifteen to thirty-three years set the Philippines apart from these two now highly urbanized and industrialized nations. It is even more interesting to note that, in the Southeast Asian context, Indonesia and Burma attained this level only in 1950, and Thailand as late as 1960.

The relatively high degree of urbanization in the Philippines early in the century may have been induced by historical circumstances. First, the Spanish colonial tradition of urbanism through "reduction"[2] meant that, for the purpose of christianization, the natives were resettled from scattered *barangays* into compact settlements (Reed, 1967:33; Phelan, 1959:55). Second, toward the end of the Spanish rule guerrilla activities became more rife in the hinterlands, forcing country people to flee to the *poblaciones.*

A slight decline in the level of urbanization from 13.1 to 12.6 percent occurred between 1903 and 1918 (Table 1). This unusual phenomenon was caused by three corollary factors. First, the departure of the Spanish administrators ended their aggressive resettlement programs; there was vehement resistance to these programs (Reed, 1967:55) to start with, so that a trickling-back of the natives to their rural hamlets seemed natural Second, peace began to reign in the countryside as Filipinos accepted American rule; this interpretation is consistent with the fact that most of the decrease in national urbanization was accounted for by a marked loss of urban population in the Central Luzon region, the foremost site of guerrilla activities before the twentieth century. Third, further encouragement for the natives to return to the farms was created by (a) the distribution to deserving farmers of friar lands for cultivation of food and other primary products (Worcester, 1914:829-845), and (b) the lifting by 1913 of export duties on farm products, such as sugar, tobacco, hemp, and copra (Abelarde, 1947:5-72).

The 1918-1939 period was pivotal in that urbanization was appreciable all over the country. The level rose to 21.6 percent, a gain of nine points

TABLE 1

Philippines: Level and Tempo of Urbanization, Urban, Rural, and Total Populations, and Respective Annual Growth Rates, 1903-1970

Year	Level (pct.)	Tempo	Urban (000's)	Pct. Change	Rural (000's)	Pct. Change	Total (000's)	Pct. Change
1903	13.1		1,000.2		6,635.2		7,635.4	
1918	12.6	-0.32	1,294.2	1.64	9,020.1	1.96	10,314.3	1.91
1939	21.6	3.36	3,450.7	5.02	12,549.6	1.66	16,000.3	2.22
1948	27.0	3.09	5,183.7	4.25	14,050.5	1.16	19,234.2	1.91
1960	29.8	1.28	8,072.5	3.98	19,015.2	2.70	27,087.7	3.06
1970	32.9	1.46	12,068.8	4.02	24,615.7	2.56	36,684.5	3.01

SOURCE: NCSO, Census on Population (various years).

in twenty-one years. The tempo of urbanization was at an all-time high as urban population growth accelerated sharply while rural growth decelerated, with total population growth picking up only slightly (Table 1). In 1939, the Philippines was more urbanized than were Thailand, Indonesia, and Burma in 1970, or South Korea in 1950. Likewise, the pace of urbanization was sharply faster in the Philippines than in the three Southeast Asian countries over the preceding twenty-year span.

The pronounced upswing in urbanization level from 1918 to 1939 was no doubt tied to socioeconomic developments during the period (Agoncillo, 1971). First a general improvement in educational standards must have spurred rural-to-urban migration. Second, the American policy of Filipinization must have opened up opportunities not only for direct employment but also for indirect participation in political and economic affairs of the provincial capitals and the *poblaciones.* Third, the Commonwealth government embarked on a strategy of industrialization and product diversification to start weaning the Philippine economy from the United States. Thus, while in 1918 there were only about five manufacturing establishments per 10,000 population, by 1939 there were eighty-seven.

Between 1939 and 1948, an interval marked by World War II and the Declaration of Independence in 1946, the speed of urbanization slowed down, although the level climbed to 27.0 percent and urban population increased from 3.4 million to 5.2 million. The decade of the 1950s saw further deceleration in the urbanization tempo as total population growth accelerated markedly. This trend can be readily seen in Table 1. Then, urbanization during the 1960s appears to have picked up somewhat as a consequence of a small drop in the rates of rural and total population increase. By 1970, 12 million Filipinos were urban, accounting for a third of the national population.[3]

The secular trend can be depicted clearly by considering two long periods in the past and the most recent decade.[4] There were periods of relatively moderate (1903-1939), rapid (1939-1960), and slow (1960-1970) tempos of urbanization, as indicated by both the urban-rural growth difference (URGD) and the percentage rise in urban proportion[5] (Table 2). The deceleration in the pace of urbanization during the latest period can be accounted for in demographic terms by the acceleration in total population growth. More specifically, whereas the urban sector absorbed a larger share of the earlier (1939-1960) acceleration in total population growth, the latest increment in the rate of growth of total population all went to the rural sector. This is evident in Table 2 which shows that, between the periods 1939-1960 and 1960-1970, the average annual growth rate picked up for total population, fell slightly for urban, but increased significantly for rural population.

The slackening in urbanization tempo occurred despite the changing pattern in internal migration from movements to frontier and rural areas earlier to urbanward transfers more recently (Smith, 1975a). In effect, therefore, gains in urban population in the way of urban in-migration and natural increase were dampened by the heightened rise in rural population resulting from its own natural increase as well as urban-rural counterstreams, as will be seen later in Chapter 5.

Against the background of slackening urbanization at the national level, urban concentration increased considerably. This is demonstrated in Table 3 by the index of primacy, which measures Metro Manila relative to the next three largest cities (Cebu, Iloilo, Bacolod). Likewise, while the smaller version of Metro Manila accounted for approximately a quarter of the nation's urban population throughout the seven decades, the larger version's share steadily inflated from a fourth to a third of total urban population (Table 4).

The distribution of urban places and population by size of place was marked at first by a concentration in one small size class and gradually diffused over only a few more lower-middle size classes in seven decades.

TABLE 2

Annual Rates of Population Growth, Urban-Rural Growth
Differences (URGD), and Percent Rise in Urban Proportion
(in percent)

	1903-1939	1939-1960	1960-1970
Total	2.09	2.52	3.01
Urban	3.52	4.10	4.02
Rural	1.79	1.99	2.56
URGD	1.73	2.11	1.46
Proportion Urban	1.40	1.54	0.97

TABLE 3

Four-City Index of First-City Primacy, 1903-1970

	1903	1939	1960	1970
Small Metro[1]	4.03	3.57	4.27	4.26
Large Metro[2]	*	*	4.91	5.31

1. Comprises the four cities of Manila, Caloocan, Pasay, Quezon, and the four municipalities of Makati, Mandaluyong, Navotas, and San Juan.
2. Comprises the small metro plus nine other municipalities. See note to Table 4.
* A large fraction of the large metro was still rural at these earlier dates.

TABLE 4

Metropolitan Manila: Level of Urbanization,
Urban Population, Share in Total Urban Population,
and Annual Growth Rate, 1903-1970

Year	Level (pct.)	Urban (000's)	Percent of Total Urban	Pct. Change
1903	76.9	256.7	25.7	
1918	87.1	371.1	28.7	2.36
1939	90.3	903.3	26.2	4.55
1948	97.1	1,526.1	29.4	5.51
1960	98.1	2,426.5	30.0	4.17
1970	100.0	3,952.6	32.8	4.90

NOTE: Metropolitan Manila comprises the four chartered cities of Manila, Caloocа Pasay, and Quezon, and the thirteen municipalities of Makati, Mandaluyong, Navotas, San Juan, Malabon, Marikina, Las Piñas, Parañaque, Pateros, Pasig, Taguig, Meycaua-yan, and Valenzuela. The total metro land area is about 610.8 square kilometers.
SOURCE: NCSO, Census on Population (various years).

(See Annex, Table A.) In 1903, about 62 percent of urban places and 50 percent of urban population were in the 2,500-5,000 size class. By 1970, only 36 percent of urban places and 24 percent of urban population were in this size class. Nonetheless, only three small size categories, 1,000-10,000, accounted for three-fourths of all urban places in 1970, while two-thirds of urban population were in the size classes 2,500-20,000. The corresponding situation in 1903 was 83 percent for urban places and 85 percent for urban population.

The Regional Patterns

Regional urbanization patterns can be conveniently and instructively presented by grouping the country's twelve regions into metropolitan, more urbanized, less urbanized, and frontier regions. The level that divides the metropolitan and more urbanized regions, on the one hand, and the less urbanized and frontier regions, on the other, is the 1960 and 1970 national average computed excluding Metro Manila.[6] The regional groupings according to their respective urbanization levels during the four major census years and the corresponding intercensal tempos are shown in Table 5, and graphed for better appreciation in Figure 1. Map 1 illustrates the geographic positions of the regions.[7]

The data lead to some noteworthy observations. First, the metro region started out already in 1903 at a much higher level (77 percent) than all other regions, urbanized very rapidly, and completed the process by 1970. Thus, as Figure 1 dramatically illustrates, it has been an urban "island" in a predominantly rural "sea." Second, the more urbanized regions, comprising Central-Southern Luzon and Western-Central Visayas, started out at a level (10 percent) lower than the less urbanized group but proceeded rapidly, particularly after 1939, reaching 30 percent in 1970. Third, the less urbanized regions of Ilocos, Bicol, and Eastern Visayas urbanized extremely sluggishly, gaining merely eight points (12 to 20 percent) throughout the entire stretch. This group of regions is characterized by consistently severe net out-migration and incomes even lower than those in the frontier regions, as will be shown in Chapter 4. Fourth, the frontier regions of Cagayan and Mindanao were the least urban in 1903 (6 percent), urbanized most rapidly up to 1939, but diminished in speed thereafter, remaining the least urban at 18 percent in 1970.[8] Finally, the national trend changes considerably when the metro region is excluded, that is, the levels are consequentially lower and the tempos slower.

The regional patterns over time further explain the faltering rhythm of national urbanization noted in the preceding section. All regions evinced

TABLE 5

Regional Urbanization Levels and Tempos, 1903-1970
(in percent)

Region	Level				Tempo[1]		
	1903	1939	1960	1970	1903-1939	1939-1960	1960-1970
Metro Manila	76.9	90.3	98.1	100.0	3.0	8.3	4.9
More Urbanized	10.1	17.5	26.7	30.5	1.9	2.6	1.9
Central Luzon	11.1	16.5	26.5	31.8	1.3	2.9	2.6
Southern Luzon	10.1	18.0	26.8	32.8	1.9	2.5	2.9
Western Visayas	13.3	21.5	30.5	27.6	1.6	2.2	-1.4
Central Visayas	5.7	13.7	22.2	28.5	2.8	2.8	3.3
Less Urbanized	12.5	16.5	19.8	20.5	0.9	1.0	0.4
Ilocos	13.8	15.9	17.6	20.6	0.5	0.6	1.9
Bicol	14.3	18.0	21.9	21.8	0.7	1.1	-0.1
Eastern Visayas	9.5	15.4	18.9	19.0	1.6	1.2	0.1
Frontier	5.8	16.2	18.6	18.3	3.4	0.8	-0.2
Cagayan	3.4	11.5	14.1	14.3	3.8	1.2	0.1
Western Mindanao	3.8	21.7	16.8	16.2	5.7	-1.6	-0.4
Northern Mindanao	12.5	15.2	20.2	18.7	0.6	1.7	-1.1
Southern Mindanao	1.6	18.1	20.9	21.5	7.8	0.9	0.4
Philippines (less Metro)	10.2	17.0	22.9	24.8	1.7	1.8	1.0
Philippines	13.1	21.6	29.8	32.9	1.7	2.1	1.5

1. Urban-rural growth difference (URGD).
SOURCE: NCSO, Census on Population (various years).

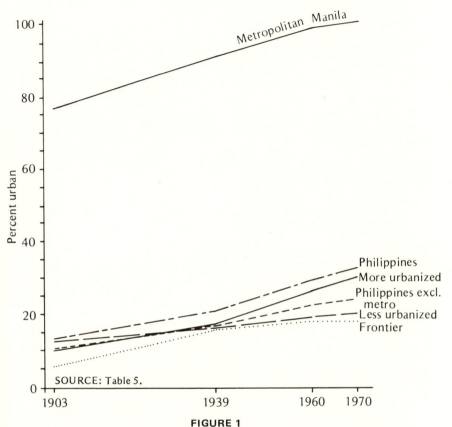

FIGURE 1

Urbanization Trends by Broad Regions and for the Country as a Whole,
1903-1970

decelerating urbanization in the 1960-1970 period; this pattern was especially pronounced for the less urbanized and frontier regions which
virtually stagnated. In 1970, these regions were five or more points below
the national (less metro) average and ten or more below the more urbanized
level. Thus, the varying urbanization rates among regions led to widening
divergence after a remarkable regional convergence at around the 17 percent
level in 1939. (See Figure 1.)

The interregional imbalance is also reflected in urban population shares
as shown in Table 6 and Figure 2. Metro Manila consistently increased
its share from a fourth to a third and, as pointed out earlier, accentuated

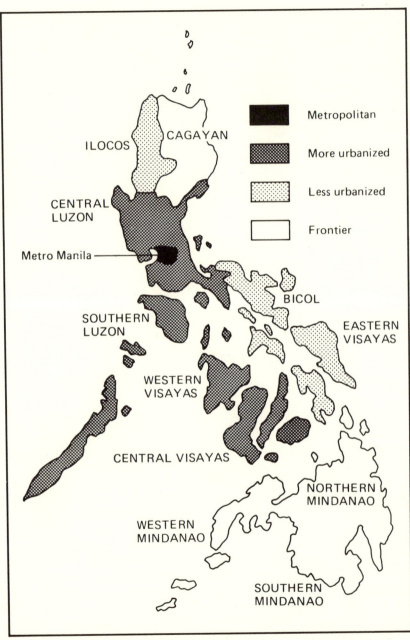

MAP 1   Philippines: Metropolitan, More Urbanized, Less Urbanized, and Frontier Regions, 1939, 1960, and 1970

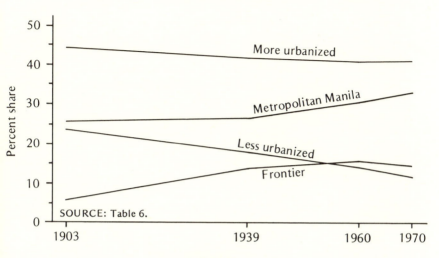

FIGURE 2

Broad Regional Shares of Urban Population, 1903-1970

TABLE 6

Broad Regional Shares of Urban Population, 1903-1970
(in percent)

Regions	1903	1939	1960	1970
Metro Manila	25.7	26.2	30.1	32.8
More Urbanized	44.3	41.8	40.7	40.8
Less Urbanized	24.4	18.1	14.0	11.8
Frontier	5.6	13.9	15.2	14.6

SOURCE: Annex, Table B.

its primacy. The more urbanized group suffered a small loss between 1903 and 1939, but practically maintained its share thereafter at about two-fifths. The less urbanized category manifested continuous diminution from just under one-fourth to just over one-ninth, again denoting the persistent loss of urban population to the metro region. The frontier group increased its urban fraction from 6 percent in 1903 to 14 percent in 1939, remaining more or less stable at that level until 1970.

The varied levels and tempos of urbanization among regions reflect differential rates of natural increase between regions and between rural and urban sectors within regions; differential rates of in- and out-migration within and between regions in terms of volume, composition, and rural-urban type; and past government policies of settlement. Underlying these differentials have been differences in socioeconomic conditions and development, which will be investigated in subsequent chapters.

A COMPARATIVE PERSPECTIVE

The Past Western Context

The long-term trend of Philippine urbanization in the twentieth century may be seen in clearer perspective if contrasted with the historical experience of developed countries at similar phases of urbanization.[9] Taking the United States and Sweden as examples, we find that what the Philippines accomplished between 1903 and 1970 (sixty-seven years), the United States did from about 1845 to 1887 (forty-two years), and Sweden from 1870 to 1930 (sixty years).[10] In other words, if the Philippines had urbanized as speedily as the United States, for example, its level of urbanization in 1970 would have been 46.6 percent, which was the United States level around 1912. The absolute growth of urban population in the Philippines, however, had been comparatively brisk. During the intervals of comparable urbanization, while urban population increased 636 percent in the United States and 270 percent in Sweden, in the Philippines it expanded 1,107 percent. If the Philippines' urban population had grown at the same rate as the American or Swedish, it would have been only 61 or 31 percent, respectively, of that observed in 1970. Yet, the actual level of urbanization in 1970 would have been attained anyway.

Since Western nations are now highly urbanized, comparing recent Philippine urbanization with their recent experience would be inappropriate. Instead, we go back to their past history and find those phases which correspond to the Philippine experience between 1950 and 1970. In other words, we determine their urbanization levels similar to the Philippine level in 1950 and then compare the tempos for the succeeding decades. Table 7 provides urbanization indices for the Philippines and selected

TABLE 7

Urbanization Indices for the Philippines and Selected Western Countries

Country Year	Level (pct. urban)	Tempo (annual)	Urban Population (thousands)	Urban Percent Change (annual)	Rural Percent Change (annual)
Philippines					
1950	27.5		5,469		
1960	29.8	1.16	8,072	3.97	2.81
1970	32.9	1.46	12,069	4.02	2.56
England & Wales					
1831	25.0		3,467		
1841	28.9	2.00	4,609	2.89	0.89
1851	35.0	2.86	6,265	3.12	0.26
France					
1856	27.3		9,845		
1866	30.5	1.57	11,595	1.65	0.08
1876	32.4	0.88	11,977	0.32	-0.56
Sweden					
1910	24.8		1,370		
1920	29.5	2.41	1,742	2.43	0.02
1930	32.5	1.41	1,996	1.37	-0.04
United States					
1870	25.7		10,233		
1880	28.2	1.31	14,144	3.29	1.98
1890	35.4	3.43	22,283	4.65	1.22

NOTE: *Urban Definitions*: Philippines—see Chapter 1; England and Wales—cities 20,000+; France—urban communes 2,000+; Sweden—towns 2,000+; and United States—places 2,500+.

SOURCES: Philippines—computed from NCSO data; England and Wales and France—Weber (1899:47 and 68); Sweden—Woytinsky and Woytinsky (1953:130) and United Nations (1948); and United States—U.S. Bureau of the Census (1973) and Woytinsky and Woytinsky (1953:124).

Western countries, namely England and Wales, and France in addition to Sweden and the United States.

In 1831, the level of urbanization in England and Wales was 25 percent, which was lower than the Philippine level in 1950. Twenty years later, England and Wales surpassed the Philippines by urbanizing at an average tempo of 2.4 percent per annum, which was almost double the Philippine rate.[11]

France's urbanization during 1856-1876 approximated the recent Philippine experience. France exhibited faster urbanization during the first decade but slower in the second, averaging 1.2 percent yearly compared to the Philippines' 1.3.

Sweden's degree of urbanization in 1910 was far below the Philippine level in 1950. Two decades later, however, Sweden was practically on the same level as the Philippines.

Finally, American urbanization between 1870 and 1890 was a marked contrast to that for the Philippines in recent years. Although the initial level for the United States was inferior, its final level was superior because of a faster pace, especially in the later decade (3.4 percent) when it was more than double the Philippine rate.

Thus, the developed nations, except France perhaps, experienced faster urbanization in the past. If, for instance, the Philippines had urbanized as fast as had England and Wales or the United States, its level in 1970 would have been about 38 instead of 33 percent. Even if the rate were just as moderate as Sweden's, it would have been 36 percent.

The rate of urban population growth, however, was materially higher in the Philippines during 1950-1970 than in the Western countries during any comparable decade, except 1880-1890 in the United States, England and Wales, which urbanized relatively rapidly, experienced an average urban growth of 3.0 percent per year compared to 4.0 percent for the Philippines. France, which urbanized at about the same tempo as the Philippines, had an average urban growth rate of one-fourth the Philippine rate. If the Philippines had had an urban growth similar to that of England and Wales, its urban population in 1970 would have been at least 17 percent smaller; if similar to France, only a little more than half the 1970 size. Yet, again, it could have urbanized as much or even more than it actually did during the past two decades.[12]

The last column of Table 7 shows the annual rates of rural population change. The Philippine rates stand out for they are multiples of the Western rates. The pronounced contrast can be seen particularly in the later decade when France and Sweden's rural populations were already declining.

Urbanization in terms of large cities (urban places of 100,000 or more population) is shown in Table 8, comparing the Philippines with England and Wales and the United States. The 1950-1970 experience of the Philippines was approximated by England and Wales in 1811-1831 and by the United States in 1880-1900. As in the previous case, the Philippines manifested slower urbanization or citification. The mean annual rates for England and Wales and the United States were 1.8 and 2.5 percent, respectively, while the rate for the Philippines was only 1.3 percent. Nevertheless, both city and noncity population growth were more buoyant for the Philippines.

The Recent Asian Context

A comparative analysis of the Philippines with Southeast Asian countries may be more meaningful inasmuch as these countries are similar in culture, development, and recent colonial experience. In Table 9 (upper panel), the Philippines is compared with Thailand, Western Malaysia, Indonesia, and Burma.

In 1950, the urban proportion of 27.5 percent in the Philippines was the most advanced in the Southeast Asian region. By 1970, however, Western Malaysia, which was three percentage points below the Philippines in 1950, became the most urbanized at 45.3 percent, twelve points above the Philippines. Thailand, Indonesia, and Burma, which were at markedly lower levels, also evinced more buoyant urbanization (except Burma's 1950-1960 experience), although they could not equal the Philippine level in 1970. (See also Figure 3.) The urban population of the Philippines was next in size to that of Indonesia, and its urban growth rate was relatively moderate. However, its rural population increase was comparatively rapid, only slightly less than Thailand's which was the fastest during the two decades.

It may be that the pace of urbanization in the Philippines was relatively slow because the initial level in 1950 was already high. This possibility can be tested by contrasting the Philippines to East Asian countries which had been more advanced in terms of both urbanization and development. The statistics for South Korea, Taiwan, and Japan are presented in the lower panel of Table 9. In 1950, Taiwan and Japan were already far advanced, but they still urbanized much more rapidly in the subsequent

TABLE 8

Citification[1] Indices for the Philippines and Selected Western Countries

Country / Year	Level (pct. city)	Tempo (annual)	City Population (thousands)	City Percent Change (annual)	Noncity Percent Change (annual)
Philippines					
1950	13.5		2,692		
1960	14.7	1.01	3,989	4.01	3.00
1970	16.7	1.55	6,140	4.32	2.77
England & Wales					
1811	12.0		1,220		
1821	13.5	1.37	1,619	2.87	1.50
1831	16.3	2.26	2,263	3.40	1.14
United States					
1880	12.4		6,219		
1890	15.4	2.60	9,694	4.54	1.94
1900	18.7	2.40	14,211	3.90	1.50

1. Citification refers to urbanization in terms of large cities or urban places of 100,000+ population.
SOURCES: Philippines—computed from NCSO (1972a); England and Wales—adapted from Weber (1899:46); and United States—U.S. Bureau of the Census (1961).

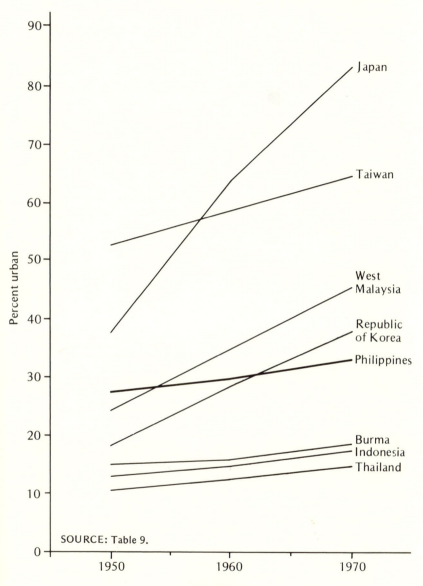

FIGURE 3
Levels of Urbanization in Southeast and East Asian Countries
1950-1970

TABLE 9

Urbanization Indices for the Philippines and Selected Asian Countries, 1950-1970

Country / Year	Level (pct. urban)	Tempo (annual)	Urban Population (thousands)	Urban Percent Change (annual)	Rural Percent Change (annual)
Philippines					
1950	27.5		5,469		
1960	29.8	1.16	8,072	3.97	2.81
1970	32.9	1.46	12,069	4.02	2.56
Thailand					
1950	10.5		2,060		
1960	12.5	2.04	3,296	4.81	2.77
1970	14.8	2.04	5,351	4.96	2.92
Western Malaysia					
1950	24.3		1,263		
1960	34.9	5.30	2,410	6.67	1.37
1970	45.3	4.49	4,138	5.55	1.06

Indonesia					
1950	12.9		9,915		
1960	14.6	1.42	13,729	3.31	1.89
1970	17.2	2.00	20,941	4.31	2.31
Burma					
1950	15.0		2,750		
1960	15.8	0.60	3,500	2.44	1.84
1970	18.5	1.99	5,137	3.91	1.92
South Korea					
1950	18.4		3,750		
1960	28.3	5.80	6,997	6.44	0.64
1970	37.9	4.51	12,175	5.70	1.19
Taiwan					
1950	52.2		3,977		
1960	58.5	2.64	6,212	4.56	1.92
1970	64.4	2.57	9,272	4.09	1.52
Japan					
1950	37.4		31,203		
1960	63.5	10.81	59,333	6.64	−4.17
1970	83.2	10.30	85,509	3.72	−6.58

SOURCE: Philippines—computed from NCSO data; Taiwan and Japan—Davis (1969:Table A); and all others—United Nations (1973a:Table 20)

periods than did the Philippines. The three East Asian countries also exhibited faster urban population growth but slower rural growth.

The urbanization differentials borne out above may possibly be attributed to different definitions of urban (although we have already commented on this matter above). Philippine urbanization might have been comparatively more rapid if a more standard definition were used for all countries compared. Also, the Philippines might have revealed faster urbanization with respect to large cities. As with the Western nations, a test for both definition and size can be made by looking into urbanization in terms of urban places with 100,000 or more inhabitants. Table 10 displays data on population and proportion in cities of 100,000 or more in the eight Asian countries for the decades 1950-1970. Again, the Philippines had the highest proportion of city population in the Southeast Asian region at the start of the period but was overtaken by Western Malaysia at the end. Except for Thailand and Burma in 1950-1960, the Philippines had the lowest rate of citification. Likewise, the rates for the more advanced East Asian countries were significantly faster. (See also Figure 4.)

Thus, in the context of a reasonably broad cross-section of countries (developing, newly developed, and long-developed), the Philippines exhibited slow urbanization. While the growth of urban population was brisk, and even more brisk than in countries whose urbanization rates were faster, rural population growth was vigorous enough to retard the rise in the urban proportion, as already demonstrated earlier in the historical survey.

SUMMARY AND CONCLUSION

Our historical analysis has revealed a number of noteworthy points. First, religious and political forces during the Spanish regime already generated a relatively high urban proportion at the outset of this century. Second, the postwar acceleration in total population growth was accompanied by a deceleration in the pace of urbanization because virtually all of the acceleration went to rural growth. Third, while the urban proportion increased only two and a half times, from about one-eighth to one-third in approximately seventy years, urban population multiplied at least twelvefold. Fourth, the more developed regions urbanized faster than the others, and urban growth unremittingly gravitated toward Manila

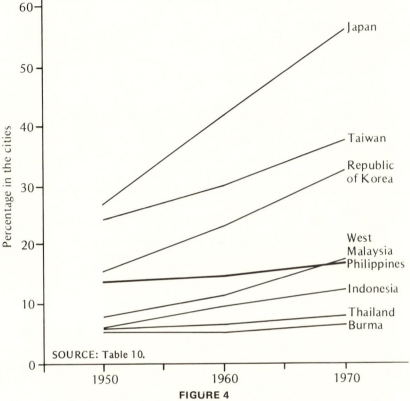

FIGURE 4

Levels of Citification in Southeast and East Asian Countries,
1950-1970

as mirrored in the continuous rise of the primacy index. Thus, apart from
the impact of large absolute increments to urban population overall, the
phenomenal expansion of Metro Manila has apparently created the illusion
of rapid urbanization.[13] In fact, Manila's dizzying growth has been con-
founding the experts' attempts to aptly define the metropolitan area.

In turn, our comparative analysis has corroborated our historical findings. First, the speed of urbanization in Western countries during the nineteenth and early twentieth centuries proved to be generally faster than
in the Philippines during the last two decades, but their urban growth
rate was slower. Second, other contemporary Southeast and East Asian
countries also evinced more rapid urbanization, particularly the fast-
developing ones.

TABLE 10

Citification[1] Indices for the Philippines and Selected Asian Countries,
1950-1970

Country / Year	Level (pct. city)	Tempo (annual)	City Population (thousands)	City Percent Change (annual)	Noncity Percent Change (annual)
Philippines					
1950	13.5		2,692		
1960	14.7	1.01	3,989	4.01	3.00
1970	16.7	1.55	6,140	4.32	2.77
Thailand					
1950	5.9		1,167		
1960	6.5	0.97	1,705	3.86	2.89
1970	7.9	2.16	2,825	5.18	3.02
Western Malaysia					
1950	7.9		409		
1960	11.2	4.06	774	6.59	2.53
1970	17.1	5.13	1,600	7.53	2.40

Indonesia					
1950	6.1		4,637		
1960	9.7	5.25	9,082	6.95	1.70
1970	12.1	2.58	14,340	4.67	2.09
Burma					
1950	5.2		977		
1960	5.3	0.27	1,194	2.03	1.76
1970	6.8	2.73	1,880	4.64	1.91
South Korea					
1950	15.2		3,124		
1960	22.8	5.17	5,707	6.21	1.04
1970	32.4	5.02	10,439	6.22	1.20
Taiwan					
1950	24.0		1,829		
1960	30.0	3.17	3,181	5.69	2.52
1970	37.6	3.55	5,420	5.47	1.92
Japan					
1950	26.6		22,218		
1960	41.9	7.04	39,180	5.84	-1.20
1970	56.3	5.83	57,850	3.97	-1.86

1. Citification refers to urbanization in terms of large cities or urban places of 100,000+ population.
SOURCES: Philippines—computed from NCSO (1972a); and all others—Davis (1969:Table A).

ANNEX

TABLE A

Philippines: Distribution of Urban Places and Population
by Size of Place, 1903, 1918, 1939, 1948, 1960, and 1970

Size-Class	1903		1918		1939	
	Number	Percent	Number	Percent	Number	Percent
			Urban Places			
500,000+						
250,000						
125,000					1	0.1
100,000					1	0.1
50,000			1	0.3	4	0.6
25,000	3	1.2	5	1.4	5	0.7
20,000					6	0.9
10,000	11	4.6	8	2.2	28	4.0
5,000	29	12.0	35	9.5	117	16.6
2,500	149	61.8	161	43.8	362	51.5
1,000	23	9.5	68	18.5	136	19.3
500	16	6.6	40	10.9	28	4.0
Under 500	10	4.1	50	13.6	15	2.1
Total	241	100.0	368	100.0	703	100.0

Urban Population

Size class	Population	%	Population	%	Population	%
500,000+						
250,000						
125,000					160,958	4.7
100,000					111,995	3.2
50,000					275,232	8.0
25,000			71,905	5.6	156,835	4.5
20,000	103,128	10.3	173,414	13.4	129,892	3.8
10,000	153,459	15.3	117,785	9.1	374,354	10.8
5,000	188,668	18.9	221,216	17.1	753,043	21.8
2,500	503,923	50.4	547,732	42.3	1,241,956	36.0
1,000	35,000	3.5	116,539	9.0	224,303	6.5
500	12,330	1.2	30,030	2.3	18,680	0.5
Under 500	3,669	0.4	15,552	1.2	3,423	0.1
Total	1,000,177	100.0	1,294,173	100.0	3,450,671	100.0

TABLE A (Continued)

Size-Class	1948		1960		1970	
	Number	Percent	Number	Percent	Number	Percent
			Urban Places			
500,000+						
250,000	1	0.1	2	0.1	2	0.1
125,000	2	0.2	1	0.1	2	0.1
100,000					2	0.1
50,000	2	0.2	9	0.6	9	0.4
25,000	10	0.9	13	0.9	28	1.2
20,000	7	0.6	23	1.5	17	0.7
10,000	49	4.5	77	5.1	163	6.9
5,000	180	16.5	252	16.6	422	17.9
2,500	463	42.4	692	45.6	837	35.5
1,000	174	16.0	297	19.6	496	21.0
500	81	7.0	85	5.6	209	8.9
Under 500	122	11.2	66	4.4	169	7.2
Total	1,091	100.0	1,517	100.0	2,356	100.0

			Urban Population			
500,000+						
250,000	283,384	5.5	639,635	7.9	788,774	6.5
125,000	373,662	7.2	127,708	1.6	265,704	2.2
100,000					232,339	1.9
50,000	126,158	2.4	622,217	7.7	522,395	4.3
25,000	360,337	7.0	458,624	5.7	889,504	7.4
20,000	155,623	3.0	513,725	6.4	393,883	3.3
10,000	642,372	12.4	1,049,016	13.0	2,153,525	17.8
5,000	1,255,580	24.2	1,706,267	21.1	2,884,678	23.9
2,500	1,597,103	30.8	2,386,004	29.6	2,900,881	24.0
1,000	295,972	5.7	487,683	6.0	825,159	6.8
500	60,699	1.2	63,018	0.8	160,025	1.3
Under 500	32,797	0.6	18,588	0.2	51,934	0.4
Total	5,183,687	100.0	8,072,485	100.0	12,068,801	100.0

SOURCE: NCSO, Census on Population (various years).

TABLE B

Urban Population and Percent Share by Regions, 1903, 1939, 1960, and 1970

Region	1903		1939		1960		1970	
	Number	Pct. Share	Number	Pct. Share	Number	Pct. Share	Number	Pct. Share
Metro Manila	256,729	25.7	903,313	26.2	2,426,488	30.1	3,952,615	32.8
More Urbanized	442,753	44.3	1,443,381	41.8	3,288,793	40.7	4,920,353	40.8
Central Luzon	140,795	14.1	379,562	11.0	958,954	11.9	1,574,089	13.0
Southern Luzon	93,938	9.4	327,546	9.5	831,257	10.3	1,484,015	12.3
Western Visayas	143,733	14.4	467,688	13.6	937,788	11.6	997,588	8.3
Central Visayas	64,287	6.4	268,585	7.8	560,794	6.9	864,661	7.2
Less Urbanized	244,300	24.4	624,433	18.1	1,132,367	14.0	1,428,065	11.8
Ilocos	90,011	9.0	156,670	4.5	229,507	2.8	329,925	2.7
Bicol	92,326	9.2	242,891	7.0	517,165	6.4	646,184	5.4
Eastern Visayas	61,963	6.2	224,872	6.5	385,695	4.8	451,956	3.7
Frontier	56,395	5.6	479,544	13.9	1,224,837	15.2	1,767,768	14.6
Cagayan	9,941	1.0	82,408	2.4	169,825	2.1	242,262	2.0
Western Mindanao	7,199	0.7	130,804	3.8	226,265	2.8	301,868	2.5
Northern Mindanao	36,238	3.6	159,384	4.6	427,330	5.3	562,969	4.7
Southern Mindanao	3,017	0.3	106,948	3.1	401,417	5.0	660,669	5.5
Philippines	1,000,177	100.0	3,450,671	100.0	8,072,485	100.0	12,068,801	100.0

SOURCE: NCSO, Census on Population (various years).

NOTES

1. Of a total population of 7.6 million, 648,000, or 8.5 percent, were considered *infieles* or uncivilized. Since they were not included in the municipal breakdowns, they could not be accounted for by the size/density urban definition. However, assuming that *infieles* (by definition) lived in the rural hinterlands, their numbers were simply included in the rural proportion in estimating provincial, regional, and national levels of urbanization.

2. The strategy of "reduction" was earlier applied to Hispanic America (Reed, 1967:35), so that countries there also exhibit levels of urbanization that are high vis-à-vis those of other developing countries.

3. The socioeconomic determinants of recent urbanization will be investigated in Chapter 4.

4. By doing this, we can also ignore the 1918 and 1948 censuses, which are not as good as the other four.

5. This is similar to what Dovring (1959) calls the "coefficient of differential growth," i.e., the rate of urbanization is simply the difference between the rates of growth for urban population and total population.

6. When Metro Manila is included in the computation, the national average becomes too high and virtually all regions fall below the average.

7. For a more detailed reference, see also the map in the Appendix.

8. The rapid pace before 1939 can be attributed to massive frontierward flows which subsequently slowed down and shifted to metropolitan and more urbanized regions.

9. Although the definitions of urban vary between countries, they are similar enough for the comparisons to make sense. Moreover, the emphasis on change in the levels or tempos of urbanization (URGD) minimizes the definitional bias. For the different urban definitions, see Davis (1969).

10. The estimates for the United States were derived by interpolation of ten-year data from the U.S. Bureau of the Census (1961). For Sweden, data are from Weber (1899:110) for 1870-1890, and the rest are from Woytinsky and Woytinsky (1953:130) and United Nations (1948).

11. It is to be noted that England and Wales' urbanization was for cities of 20,000 or more; for smaller urban places it may even have been faster.

12. Therefore, this patently indicates that, contrary to common impression, rapid urban population growth does not necessarily generate a correspondingly rapid urbanization (see also Davis, 1965 and 1972).

13. Manila has, of course, been the center of attraction and attention of sorts, so that Philippine urbanization has become synonymous with its growth. See also Jones (1972).

COMPONENTS OF URBAN POPULATION GROWTH

3

Allied to the notion of rapid urbanization has been the belief that urban places and cities have been growing largely as a consequence of rural-urban migration. This belief is evident, for example, in the works of Murphey (1966) and Myrdal (1968) on Asia, or in those of Durand and Pelaez (1965) and Artle (1970) on Latin America. While there has been no systematic study as yet on the sources of urban population growth in the Philippines, a similar impression has imbued statements regarding the impact of rural-urban migration on urbanization there.

The growth of urban population can stem from three sources, namely, natural increase, net rural-urban migration, and net rural-to-urban reclassification of places.[1] In this chapter, we attempt to estimate the components of urban growth or analyze the extent to which each of the three sources contributed to urban growth during the past seventy years.

First, we present the estimation procedures. Next, we apply the procedures to municipal census data and aggregate the results to the provincial, regional, and national levels. Then, we discuss the national and regional results, leaving the provincial results to the Appendix. In addition, we examine the growth components of major cities using a direct procedure with census migration data.

THE METHOD

We start with a balancing equation expressing the components of urban growth

$$UG = NR + NI + NM \tag{1}$$

where

UG = urban population growth from t to $t + n$,

NR = net reclassification of places from rural to urban,

NI = natural increase during the interval, and

NM = net migration into urban areas during the interval.

Net reclassification is the difference between positive reclassification and negative reclassification. Positive reclassification refers to the upgrading of a place from rural to urban when it meets the population size, density, or contiguity criteria; negative reclassification is the reverse process.[2]

In estimating the right-hand side of equation (1), we adopt the following steps:

Step 1: We establish constant urban boundaries by identifying places that were urban both at the start and at the end of a period under consideration. New urban places found at the end of the period are considered as urban gain due to positive reclassification (R^+). In other words,

$$R^+ = P_{t+n} - \bar{P}_{t+n}, \quad (P_{t+n} > \bar{P}_{t+n}) \tag{2}$$

where P_{t+n} refers to urban population observed at the end of the period, and $\bar{P}_{t+n}$ to urban population within constant boundaries also at the end of the period. On the other hand, places that cease to be urban at the end of the period are regarded as urban loss due to negative reclassification (R^-). Or, algebraically,

$$R^- = P_{t+n} - \bar{P}_{t+n}, \quad (P_{t+n} < \bar{P}_{t+n}). \tag{3}$$

Net reclassification (NR)

$$NR = P_{t+n} - \bar{P}_{t+n} \tag{4}$$

can, therefore, be positive, negative, or zero depending on whether R+ is greater than, less than, or equal to R— for a given municipality, province, region, or the whole country.

Step 2: We project the initial urban population within constant boundaries to the end of the period using the formula $\hat{\bar{P}}_{t+n} = \bar{P}_t (1 + r)^n$.

Urban population growth resulting from natural increase is simply the difference between the projected and the initial populations, that is,

$$NI = \hat{\bar{P}}_{t+n} - \bar{P}_t. \tag{5}$$

For the rate of natural increase (r), we use two different rates appropriate for urban areas and for Metropolitan Manila, as explained in the Annex to this chapter.

Step 3: Finally, net migration into urban areas can be indirectly calculated by taking the difference between urban populations enumerated and expected within constant boundaries at the end of the period, that is,

$$NM = \bar{P}_{t+n} - \hat{\bar{P}}_{t+n}. \tag{6}$$

It should be noted that the net migration estimate includes whatever natural reproduction occurs to the in-migrants during the interval.[3]

Equation (1) can now be reformulated employing formulae (4) to (6). Thus,

$$UG = (P_{t+n} - \bar{P}_{t+n}) + (\hat{\bar{P}}_{t+n} - \bar{P}_t) + (\bar{P}_{t+n} - \hat{\bar{P}}_{t+n}). \tag{7}$$

Removing the parentheses, equation (7) reduces to

$$UG = P_{t+n} - \bar{P}_t \tag{8}$$

which merely expresses the difference between the initial urban population within constant boundaries and the final urban population observed both inside and outside the boundaries.

Net reclassification can be further decomposed into three elements

$$NR = RP_t + NI + NM \tag{9}$$

where RP_t refers to the population of places that were rural at the start of the period; and NI and NM constitute the incremental populations (from natural increase and net migration, respectively) that made formerly rural places qualify as urban. NI can be estimated as $\hat{RP}_{t+n} - RP_t$, and NM can be approximated as $RP_{t+n} - \hat{RP}_{t+n}$. In order to derive $\hat{RP}_{t+n}$, we utilize rates of natural increase (r) appropriate for rural areas. (See Annex to this chapter.) Therefore, equation (9) can be restated as

$$NR = RP_t + (\widehat{RP}_{t+n} - RP_t) + (RP_{t+n} - \widehat{RP}_{t+n}) \qquad (10)$$

which reduces to $NR = RP_{t+n}$. In other words, net reclassification simply refers to the end-of-the-period population of places that were previously outside urban boundaries but have now come within expanded urban boundaries.

Consequently, the two procedures involving the decomposition of urban growth and then of net reclassification produce two natural increase components as well as two net migration components. As a final procedure, we can estimate combined or aggregate natural increase and aggregate net migration components, in which case our original equation (1) becomes

$$UG = RP_t + NI^* + NM^* \qquad (11)$$

where RP_t is the basic rural population that becomes reclassified as urban, identical to that in equation (9), and the asterisks denote combined estimates, i.e., $NI^* > NI$, and $NM^* > NM$. Equation (11) enables us to assess the full impact of rural-urban migration vis-à-vis urban natural reproduction on the growth of urban population.[4]

THE RESULTS

We apply the method to Philippine census data over two long intervals in the past, 1903-1939 and 1939-1960, and the most recent intercensal period, 1960-1970. This involves looking at places (*barrios* and *poblaciones*) in each municipality. The populations of these places may be aggregated to the provincial and regional levels, from which may be derived national estimates. The tables below present the estimates of urban growth components at the national and regional levels, following in the order of the three estimation procedures of the method. As already noted, these estimates are based on the municipal and provincial results, which are given in the Appendix.

Tables 11-13 show the components of urban growth for the Philippines and its regions during the three different periods, as estimated according to the three steps of the first procedure. Over the period 1903-1939 (Table 11), the largest component of national urban growth was net reclassification (67.7 percent), followed by natural increase (35.7 percent), and net migration (–3.4 percent). For most regions, urban growth was

TABLE 11

Components of Urban Growth at National and Regional Levels,
1903-1939 (percent distribution)

Country/Regions	Net Reclassification	Natural Increase	Net Migration	Urban Growth (100 pct.)
PHILIPPINES	67.7	35.7	-3.4	2,450,494
Metro Manila	33.9	55.1	11.0	646,584
More Urbanized	73.8	30.8	-4.6	1,000,628
Central Luzon	85.8	35.8	-21.6	238,767
Southern Luzon	75.5	29.7	-5.3	233,608
Western Visayas	71.9	33.7	-5.6	323,955
Central Visayas	60.7	21.7	17.6	204,298
Less Urbanized	85.2	46.7	-31.9	380,133
Ilocos	93.1	101.6	-94.6	66,659
Bicol	85.2	42.5	-27.7	150,565
Eastern Visayas	81.9	28.1	-10.0	162,909
Frontier	89.4	7.8	2.7	423,149
Cagayan	69.6	10.6	19.7	72,467
Western Mindanao	90.5	4.5	5.0	123,605
Northern Mindanao	91.1	16.2	-7.2	123,146
Southern Mindanao	100.0	0.0	0.0	103,931

Note: The broad regional groupings are based on the 1960 and 1970 regional urbanization levels, as explained in Chapter 2.

also largely accounted for by net reclassification, ranging from 34 percent for Metro Manila to 100 percent for Southern Mindanao. Net out-movement from urban areas was especially pronounced for the less urbanized regions. Of the twelve regions, seven lost urban population as a result of migration. The frontier regions as a whole and Metro Manila gained through migration, but even this increase was slight compared to the net reclassification and natural increase components.

Between 1939 and 1960 (Table 12), the net reclassification component diminished to less than half (45.4 percent) of urban growth for the country as a whole. Net migration gained some prominence at 15.5 percent, but natural increase rose slightly to just under two-fifths (39.1 percent). The largest share of metropolitan growth came from net migration (47.2 percent). In the other regions, however, gains from net migration were relatively small, and one-half of the regions saw net out-migration. In most regions, the contribution of natural increase was larger than in the previous period.

During the most recent decade, 1960-1970 (Table 13), net reclassification appears to have dropped further in importance (only 28.2 percent), while natural increase attained still greater relative dominance (54.2 percent) at the national level, and even in Metro Manila (54.3 percent). A similar pattern obtained in virtually all regions. Net migration, however, became more significant, especially in the more urbanized (10.0 percent) and frontier (16.5 percent) regions. All three less urbanized regions lost urban population through migration, but their urban growth continued to be generated by natural increase as well as net reclassification.

A further decomposition of the reclassification portion of urban growth (second procedure) is given in Tables 14-16 for the three periods. Between 1903 and 1939 (Table 14), natural increase was the most instrumental (38.4 percent) in bringing about the overall reclassification of places from rural to urban; the remainder was evenly contributed by net migration and the basic rural population (30.8 percent each). Natural increase was also relatively material in the more urbanized and less urbanized regions—as high as 66.1 percent in Central Luzon. While net migration loomed large in Metro Manila (66.0 percent), Ilocos (77.7 percent), Western Mindanao (75.2 percent), and Southern Mindanao (92.1 percent), it was negative in Central and Southern Luzon.

Over 1939 to 1960 (Table 15), the basic rural population was prominent (47.8 percent) at the national level, the share of natural increase

TABLE 12

Components of Urban Growth at National and Regional Levels, 1939-1960 (percent distribution)

Country/Regions	Net Reclassification	Natural Increase	Net Migration	Urban Growth (100 pct.)
PHILIPPINES	45.4	39.1	15.5	4,621,814
Metro Manila	9.0	43.8	47.2	1,523,175
More Urbanized	62.6	36.1	1.2	1,845,412
Central Luzon	82.2	26.5	-8.7	579,392
Southern Luzon	60.4	32.9	6.7	503,711
Western Visayas	48.7	47.9	3.4	470,100
Central Visayas	50.0	41.9	8.1	292,209
Less Urbanized	53.5	55.1	-8.6	507,934
Ilocos	43.7	93.6	-37.3	72,837
Bicol	54.3	38.6	7.2	274,274
Eastern Visayas	56.7	65.8	-22.5	160,823
Frontier	71.8	25.8	2.4	745,293
Cagayan	90.3	38.7	-29.0	87,417
Western Mindanao	60.9	49.1	-10.0	95,461
Northern Mindanao	75.7	25.1	-0.9	267,946
Southern Mindanao	66.4	15.0	18.6	294,469

TABLE 13

Components of Urban Growth at National and Regional Levels,
1960-1970 (percent distribution)

Country/Regions	Net Reclassification	Natural Increase	Net Migration	Urban Growth (100 pct.)
PHILIPPINES	28.2	54.2	17.6	3,996,316
Metro Manila	8.2	54.3	37.5	1,526,127
More Urbanized	42.3	47.6	10.0	1,631,560
Central Luzon	55.6	36.2	8.1	615,135
Southern Luzon	52.5	33.9	13.6	652,758
Western Visayas	-245.6	324.1	21.5	59,800
Central Visayas	50.3	45.7	4.0	303,867
Less Urbanized	46.7	93.8	-40.5	295,698
Ilocos	50.9	56.1	-7.1	100,418
Bicol	64.1	97.3	-61.3	129,019
Eastern Visayas	6.4	144.3	-50.7	66,261
Frontier	31.6	51.9	16.5	542,931
Cagayan	15.8	52.5	31.7	72,437
Western Mindanao	40.8	68.7	-9.5	75,603
Northern Mindanao	31.4	65.3	3.3	135,639
Southern Mindanao	33.5	39.9	26.6	259,252

TABLE 14

Components of the Net Reclassification Portion of Urban Growth
at National and Regional Levels, 1903-1939 (percent distribution)

Country/Regions	Basic Rural Population	Natural Increase	Net Migration	Net Reclassification (100 pct.)
PHILIPPINES	30.8	38.4	30.8	1,659,739
Metro Manila	15.2	18.9	66.0	219,300
More Urbanized	41.2	51.3	7.4	738,220
Central Luzon	53.1	66.1	−19.2	204,939
Southern Luzon	46.9	58.3	−5.2	176,449
Western Visayas	25.8	32.1	42.2	232,847
Central Visayas	42.6	53.0	4.3	123,985
Less Urbanized	29.2	36.3	34.5	323,854
Ilocos	9.9	12.4	77.7	62,038
Bicol	34.5	42.9	22.7	128,388
Eastern Visayas	33.1	41.1	25.8	133,428
Frontier	21.0	26.1	52.9	378,365
Cagayan	34.6	43.0	22.4	50,466
Western Mindanao	11.0	13.7	75.2	111,801
Northern Mindanao	41.0	51.0	8.0	112,167
Southern Mindanao	3.5	4.4	92.1	103,931

Note: The broad regional groupings are based on the 1960 and 1970 regional urbanization levels, as explained in Chapter 2.

TABLE 16

Components of the Net Reclassification Portion of Urban Growth
at National and Regional Levels, 1939-1960 (percent distribution)

Country/Regions	Basic Rural Population	Natural Increase	Net Migration	Net Reclassification (100 pct.)
PHILIPPINES	47.8	36.7	15.4	2,100,240
Metro Manila	34.8	26.8	38.4	137,272
More Urbanized	48.7	37.4	13.8	1,155,582
Central Luzon	48.6	37.4	14.0	476,356
Southern Luzon	46.3	35.6	18.1	304,325
Western Visayas	54.7	42.1	3.2	228,789
Central Visayas	44.7	34.4	20.9	146,112
Less Urbanized	67.2	51.6	-18.8	271,937
Ilocos	117.1	90.0	-107.1	31,839
Bicol	54.6	41.9	3.5	148,841
Eastern Visayas	70.3	54.0	-24.3	91,257
Frontier	39.4	30.3	30.4	535,449
Cagayan	40.5	31.2	28.3	78,943
Western Mindanao	68.3	52.5	-20.8	58,113
Northern Mindanao	39.9	30.7	29.4	202,943
Southern Mindanao	29.7	22.9	47.4	195,450

was about the same (36.7 percent), but net migration fell to half (15.4 percent) of what it was in the preceding interval. The national pattern was more or less replicated at the regional level, except that the less urbanized regions manifested a negative contribution from migration (–18.8 percent). Metro Manila and the frontier regions continued to experience relatively large gains from migration.

During the 1960-1970 interval (Table 16), the basic rural population loomed larger still at 89.5 percent overall, implying that in 1960 many places were already on the verge of becoming urban. Natural increase practically maintained its share at 34.5 percent, and net migration was –24.0 percent. The dominant relative share of basic rural population in net reclassification was also true for the different regions, except for Metro Manila and Western Visayas which gained much from migration. The majority of the regions appear to have experienced negative reclassification as a result of out-migration from urban areas to the metropolitan area.

To appreciate the full relative impacts of natural increase and net migration on urban growth, we now combine the estimates from the two decomposition procedures following equation (11) above, that is, the third and final procedure. The results for the three periods considered are provided in Tables 17-19. National urban growth over the period 1903-1939 (Table 17) was largely accounted for by natural increase in urban areas (61.7 percent). The contribution of net migration was only 17.4 percent, and 20.9 percent came from rural places which were reclassified into urban. Migrants accounted for one-third of metropolitan growth, and newly born urbanites constituted practically the remainder of this growth. Natural increase likewise contributed large shares to regional urban growth, except in the frontier regions which were the recipients of large numbers of migrants (as high as 92.1 percent in Southern Mindanao but zero in Northern Mindanao). Net migration's share was either small or negative, especially in the less urbanized regions.

In the next period, 1939-1960 (Table 18), natural increase was still relatively large overall (55.8 percent), although the share from net migration increased somewhat (22.5 percent). Migration explained one-half of metropolitan growth, but it was negative (–18.6 percent) in the less urbanized group and relatively minor in the more urbanized (9.9 percent) and frontier (24.2 percent) regions. Only Southern Mindanao approximated metropolitan growth because of migrants; in Ilocos it was –84.1 percent.

TABLE 16

Components of the Net Reclassification Portion of Urban Growth
at National and Regional Levels, 1960-1970 (percent distribution)

Country/Regions	Basic Rural Population	Natural Increase	Net Migration	Net Reclassification (100 pct.)
PHILIPPINES	89.5	34.5	−24.0	1,125,235
Metro Manila	33.4	12.9	53.7	124,815
More Urbanized	92.5	35.7	−28.1	690,828
Central Luzon	74.4	28.7	−3.1	342,145
Southern Luzon	61.5	23.7	14.8	342,787
Western Visayas	−38.8	−14.9	153.7	−146,860
Central Visayas	76.3	29.4	−5.7	152,756
Less Urbanized	90.7	35.0	−25.6	138,040
Ilocos	86.6	33.4	−20.0	51,159
Bicol	74.6	28.8	−3.4	82,659
Eastern Visayas	454.7	175.3	−530.1	4,222
Frontier	117.2	45.2	−62.4	171,552
Cagayan	183.8	70.9	−154.7	11,424
Western Mindanao	75.9	29.3	−5.2	30,803
Northern Mindanao	208.9	80.6	−189.5	42,542
Southern Mindanao	78.2	30.1	−8.3	86,783

TABLE 17

Aggregated Components of Urban Growth at National and Regional Levels, 1903-1939 (percent distribution)

Country/Regions	Basic RP[1]	Aggregate NI[2]	Aggregate NM[3]	Urban Growth (100 pct.)
PHILIPPINES	20.9	61.7	17.4	2,450,494
Metro Manila	5.1	61.5	33.4	646,584
More Urbanized	30.4	68.7	0.9	1,000,628
Central Luzon	45.6	92.5	-38.1	238,767
Southern Luzon	35.4	73.8	-9.2	233,608
Western Visayas	18.5	56.8	24.7	323,955
Central Visayas	25.9	53.9	20.3	204,298
Less Urbanized	24.9	77.6	-2.5	380,133
Ilocos	9.2	113.1	-22.3	66,659
Bicol	29.4	79.0	-8.4	150,565
Eastern Visayas	27.1	61.8	11.1	162,909
Frontier	18.8	31.2	50.0	423,149
Cagayan	24.1	40.6	35.4	72,467
Western Mindanao	10.0	16.9	73.1	123,605
Northern Mindanao	37.4	62.6	0.0	123,146
Southern Mindanao	3.5	4.4	92.1	103,931

1. Basic RP refers to the original rural population at the start of the period.
2. Aggregate NI refers to the combined natural increase from the first and second decompositions.
3. Aggregate NM refers to the combined net migration from the first and second decompositions.
Note: The broad regional groupings are based on the 1960 and 1970 regional urbanization levels, as explained in Chapter 2.

TABLE 18

Aggregated Components of Urban Growth at National and Regional Levels,
1939-1960 (percent distribution)

Country/Regions	Basic RP	Aggregate NI	Aggregate NM	Urban Growth (100 pct.)
PHILIPPINES	21.7	55.8	22.5	4,621,814
Metro Manila	3.1	46.2	50.7	1,523,175
More Urbanized	30.5	59.6	9.9	1,845,412
Central Luzon	40.0	57.2	2.8	579,392
Southern Luzon	28.0	54.4	17.6	503,711
Western Visayas	26.6	68.4	5.0	470,100
Central Visayas	22.4	59.1	18.6	292,209
Less Urbanized	36.0	82.7	−18.6	507,934
Ilocos	51.2	132.9	84.1	72,837
Bicol	29.6	61.3	9.1	274,274
Eastern Visayas	39.9	96.4	36.3	160,823
Frontier	28.3	47.5	24.2	745,293
Cagayan	36.6	66.9	−3.5	87,417
Western Mindanao	41.6	81.0	−22.6	95,461
Northern Mindanao	30.2	48.4	21.4	267,946
Southern Mindanao	19.7	30.2	50.1	294,469

The impact of rural-urban migration on national urban growth was the smallest (10.9 percent) during the most recent period, 1960-1970 (Table 19). This finding accords with a slow urbanization rate during the same period as seen in the previous chapter. Natural reproduction in urban areas was more marked (63.9 percent) and reclassification accounted for one-quarter of urban growth, which was slightly more than in the earlier periods. Just over two out of five additional metropolitan residents were migrants; the rest were born in the metro region. The impact of migration on urban growth was negative for all three regional groupings, particularly the less urbanized group (–52.5 percent). Five out of the twelve regions lost urban population through out-migration. The share attributable to natural reproduction was especially prominent in Western and Eastern Visayas, regions that suffered severe urban out-migration.

In sum, net rural-urban migration seems to have been a relatively insignificant factor in overall urban growth during the past seventy years. The gain from rural-urban migration loomed largest between 1939 and 1960, the period of most rapid urbanization, but during the most recent interval, it declined to an all-time low as natural increase further enlarged its share. Migration made an important contribution to metropolitan growth throughout the past seventy years, but in the other regions natural increase and reclassification were more significant.

CITY POPULATION GROWTH

We extend the analysis of urban growth by looking at the relative impact of migration on the individual growth of major cities.[5] For our purpose, major cities refer to municipalities which by 1970 had populations of 100,000 or over. These places were and are likely to continue as the principal destinations of urban in-migrants. Unlike our procedure in the previous sections where we had to utilize an indirect method for decomposing urban growth, here we can measure the components of city growth by a direct approach to the migration data of the 1970 Census. Because migration data at the municipality level are not available from the earlier censuses, we confine our analysis in this section to the 1960-1970 period.

Table 20 presents the populations of nineteen major cities in 1960 and 1970 (constant boundaries), ranked from biggest to smallest as of 1960, and their annual rates of growth during the period. All of the cities,

TABLE 19

Aggregated Components of Urban Growth at National and Regional Levels,
1960-1970 (percent distribution)

Country/Regions	Basic RP	Aggregate NI	Aggregate NM	Urban Growth (100 pct.)
PHILIPPINES	25.2	63.9	10.9	3,996,316
Metro Manila	2.7	55.4	41.9	1,526,127
More Urbanized	39.2	62.7	-1.9	1,631,560
Central Luzon	41.4	52.2	6.4	615,135
Southern Luzon	32.3	46.4	21.4	652,758
Western Visayas	95.2	360.8	-356.0	59,800
Central Visayas	38.4	60.5	1.1	303,867
Less Urbanized	42.3	110.2	-52.5	295,698
Ilocos	44.1	73.1	-17.2	100,418
Bicol	47.8	115.7	63.5	129,019
Eastern Visayas	29.0	155.5	-84.5	66,261
Frontier	37.0	66.2	-3.3	542,931
Cagayan	29.0	63.7	7.3	72,437
Western Mindanao	30.9	80.6	-11.6	75,603
Northern Mindanao	65.5	90.6	-56.1	135,639
Southern Mindanao	26.2	50.0	23.9	259,252

TABLE 20

Population of Major Cities,[1] 1960 and 1970,
and Annual Growth Rates, 1960-1970

City	1960	1970	Annual Pct. Change 1960-1970
1. Manila & Suburbs[2]	2,107,079	3,168,105	4.1
2. Cebu	251,146	347,116	3.2
3. Davao	225,712	392,473	5.6
4. Basilan	155,712	143,829	−0.8
5. Iloilo	151,266	209,738	3.2
6. Zamboanga	131,489	199,901	4.2
7. Bacolod	119,315	187,300	4.5
8. Tarlac[3]	98,285	135,128	3.2
9. Cadiz	88,542	124,108	3.4
10. Batangas	82,627	108,868	2.7
11. Butuan	79,770	131,094	5.0
12. Malabon[4]	76,438	141,514	6.2
13. Angeles	75,900	134,544	5.8
14. San Pablo	70,680	105,517	4.0
15. Cagayan de Oro	68,274	128,319	6.4
16. Pasig[4]	62,130	156,492	9.5
17. Iligan	58,433	104,493	5.9
18. Olongapo	45,330	107,785	8.9
19. Marikina[4]	40,455	113,400	10.6
TOTAL	3,988,583	6,139,724	4.3

1. Having populations of 100,000 or over by 1970.

2. Comprises Manila, Caloocan, Pasay, Quezon, Makati, Mandaluyong, Navotas, and San Juan. This is the small metro referred to in Table 3 (Chapter 2), not the metro of the preceding section.

3. Not a chartered city.

4. Not chartered cities but parts of the bigger Metropolitan Manila area.

SOURCE: NCSO (1972b).

except Basilan (which saw a decline) and Batangas, evinced annual growth rates above the national average of 3.0 percent. Excepting Malabon, Pasig, and Marikina, which are parts of the larger Metropolitan Manila area analyzed earlier, the fastest growing cities were Davao, Angeles, Cagayan de Oro, Iligan, and Olongapo where growth rates ranged 5.6 to 8.9 percent per annum. These compared with Greater Manila's (Manila and suburbs) growth rate of 4.1 percent and the weighted average growth rate for all nineteen cities of 4.3 percent.

Table 21 shows the domestic and foreign migrants ten years of age and over in the major cities between 1960 and 1970. Of the total of about 1.1 million domestic in-migrants, 61 percent were in Greater Manila, and this goes up to 70 percent when in-migrants in Malabon, Pasig, and Marikina are reckoned in the metropolitan share. Bigger cities, such as Cebu, Davao, and Bacolod also received relatively large numbers of in-migrants. The vast majority of foreign in-migrants went to Greater Manila (62 percent), but large shares were also found in Angeles and Olongapo where American military bases are situated.

Table 21 further illustrates the relative impact of migration from all places on the growth of the cities. On the average, a little over two out of three new residents above ten years of age in these cities were migrants. This was because migration accounted for an appreciable share of growth in Greater Manila (82 percent) and in the other bigger cities of Cebu (70 percent), Bacolod (58 percent), Butuan (66 percent), Cagayan de Oro (58 percent), and the military base city of Olongapo (77 percent). In the other cities, except the three satellite cities of Manila, about half or less of their growth was attributable to migration. Foreign in-migrants constituted a neglibible proportion of city growth except in Angeles and Olongapo.

SUMMARY AND CONCLUSION

Early urban population growth in this century seems to have been promoted predominantly by the reclassification of places from rural to urban, as may be expected theoretically. Later, the natural increase component became more prominent. Throughout the past seven decades, net rural-to-urban migration was a minor contributor to urban growth except in Metropolitan Manila. A further breakdown of the net reclassification factor to derive full estimates of natural increase and net migration revealed that natural increase was responsible for roughly three-fifths (56 to 64 percent) of national urban growth; net migration's share averaged only one-sixth, or less than a third of natural reproduction's

TABLE 21

Migrants 10 Years Old and Over in Major Cities and as Proportions of Population Change 10 Years Old and Over, 1960-1970

City	In-Migrants		As Pct. of Population Change		
	Domestic	Foreign	Domestic	Foreign	Total
1. Manila & Suburbs	676,878	9,541	81.6	1.1	82.7
2. Cebu	52,553	310	69.9	0.4	70.3
3. Davao	58,689	61	47.0	0.1	47.1
4. Basilan	8,426	31	-112.4	-0.4	-112.8
5. Iloilo	22,573	423	49.6	0.9	50.5
6. Zamboanga	14,316	32	31.8	0.1	31.9
7. Bacolod	29,098	30	58.2	0.1	58.3
8. Tarlac	6,822	2	24.6	0.0	24.6
9. Cadiz	11,292	0	40.1	0.0	40.1
10. Batangas	3,641	0	15.3	0.0	15.3
11. Butuan	21,840	29	65.7	0.1	65.8
12. Malabon	30,119	124	62.6	0.2	62.8
13. Angeles	17,148	2,882	43.1	7.3	50.4
14. San Pablo	5,676	29	19.4	0.1	19.5
15. Cagayan de Oro	25,250	127	57.6	0.3	57.9
16. Pasig	40,905	60	61.9	0.1	62.0
17. Iligan	17,537	72	51.3	0.2	51.5
18. Olongapo	33,046	1,576	73.3	3.5	76.8
19. Marikina	34,848	78	66.2	0.1	66.3
TOTAL	1,110,657	15,407	67.9	0.9	68.9

SOURCES: NCSO, 1960 and 1970 censuses.

share. Migration contributed substantially (about 50 percent) to metro-politan growth. In the other regions, however, migration's relative impact on urban growth was generally minor. Between regions, urban in-migra-tion was more palpable in the more urbanized and frontier (least ur-banized) regions than in the less urbanized ones which, as we shall see later on, suffered heavy out-migration. In short, at the national and regional levels, the rise in urban population and urban proportion did not involve a great deal of rural-urban mobility as fertility stayed high and mortality declined drastically in urban areas.

Migration (from all areas, not just rural areas) had a significant impact, as may be expected, on the growth of the bigger cities during the 1960s (over 50 percent). For the smaller cities, however, natural increase was the chief generator of growth. A similar finding was reported on city growth in Chile, Mexico, and Venezuela (Arriaga, 1968). This common occurrence in less developed countries has been a stark contrast to the historical experience of the developed countries. Cities in the nineteenth century, in the words of Adna Weber (1899:155), "depended almost en-tirely upon the influx of country people for their growth; mortality was so high that the deaths annually equalled or exceeded in number the births."[6] It may be concluded, therefore, that it is erroneous to grossly equate Philippine urbanization with rural-to-urban migration, as in the developed countries in the past.

ANNEX

DERIVATION OF METROPOLITAN, URBAN, AND RURAL RATES OF NATURAL INCREASE

This section illustrates the method for estimating the metropolitan, urban, and rural rates of natural increase used to compute the natural increase and migration components of urban growth.

Age specific fertility rates (ASFRs) for metropolitan, other urban, and rural sectors in 1970 can be derived from the 1973 NDS (Smith, 1975b). Using these different ASFRs, together with 1970 Census population data, we can obtain the corresponding crude birth rates (CBRs) as follows:

Metropolitan	36.33
Other Urban	35.10
Rural	44.81
National	41.87

Applying the Brass technique to children ever born (CEB) and children still living (CSL) data, also from the 1973 NDS, we can derive mortality levels for metropolitan, other urban, and rural sectors (Smith, et al., 1975). We then get the corresponding (interpolated) central death rates $(n^m x)$ from the "West" model life tables and apply them to the metropolitan, other urban, and rural age structures of the 1970 Census. Summing up the number of deaths for each age group and dividing by the total population of each sector, we obtain the following crude death rates (CDRs):

Metropolitan	6.63
Other Urban	9.38
Rural	11.10
National	10.55

While the CBR estimates are plausible, the CDRs are probably somewhat on the low side. Nonetheless, the relative intersectoral differences are reasonably indicative.

Since we are analyzing the components of urban population growth during the periods 1903-1939, 1939-1960, and 1960-1970, we need average annual rates of natural increase during these intervals for the metropolitan, other urban, and rural sectors. We start with the CBR in 1903 of about 50.0 (Smith, 1975c:84-88) and in 1970 of approximately 42.0 (as shown above). We interpolate the CBRs for the midpoints of the intervals, viz. 1921, 1949, and 1965, and calculate corresponding crude rates of natural increase (CRNIs). Thus, we get crude rates for the country as a whole:

Year	CBR	–	CRNI	=	CDR
1921	47.87	–	20.86	=	27.01
1949	44.47	–	25.23	=	19.24
1965	43.00	–	30.12	=	12.88

With the national CBRs and CDRs as benchmarks, we can now estimate our needed CRNIs for the three sectors by utilizing the relative inter-sectoral differences in fertility and mortality observed for 1970, as shown above. The estimated sectoral crude rates for the three periods are the following:

1903-1939

Sector	CBR	–	CDR	=	CRNI
Metropolitan	41.53	–	16.96	=	24.57
Other Urban	40.13	–	24.00	=	16.13
Rural	51.23	–	28.42	=	22.81

1939-1960

Sector	CBR	–	CDR	=	CRNI
Metropolitan	38.59	–	12.08	=	26.51
Other Urban	37.28	–	17.10	=	20.18
Rural	47.60	–	20.25	=	27.35

1960-1970

Sector	CBR	–	CDR	=	CRNI
Metropolitan	37.31	–	8.09	=	29.22
Other Urban	36.05	–	11.45	=	24.60
Rural	46.02	–	13.55	=	32.47

The underlying assumption is that the relative intersectoral differences observed in 1970 also obtained in the earlier periods. This is obviously a drawback in the procedure which should be borne in mind in interpreting the results. To the extent that the decline of urban mortality was faster than the decline of rural mortality, the role of natural increase in urban areas at earlier times would tend to be exaggerated.

NOTES

1. Theoretically, a fourth source is international migration, but since this has been practically inconsequential in the Philippines, we ignore it here.

2. These reclassifications can occur over time because of the nature of the urban definition, which was spelled out in Chapter 1. Positive reclassification takes place by graduation or absorption. Absorption is the process whereby a place becomes part of a bigger urban place or cluster. A place refers to a *barrio* or *poblacion;* several *barrios* and a *poblacion* make up a municipality, which is analogous to a county in the United States.

3. There is no attempt here to isolate the interaction effect: for example, migration may enhance the fertility of urban areas by the entry of women of reproductive ages, or depress it if migrants generally have lower fertility or marry later than native urbanites.

4. The above procedures become clearer as one goes through text Tables 11 to 19 and especially through Appendix Tables 1 to 9.

5. Here we deal not with rural-urban migration but with migration into individual cities from all other places whether rural, urban, or city.

6. For example, John Graunt estimated that the ratio of deaths to births was 14 to 13 in seventeenth-century London as against 52 to 63 in the countryside, implying some amount of rural-urban migration needed to maintain London's population (Keyfitz, 1972:45).

URBANIZATION AND ECONOMIC DEVELOPMENT

4

Urbanization has been observed to be closely tied to economic development in the history of advanced nations (Lampard, 1955). It was quite natural for labor and the population in general to shift constantly from the rural to the urban sector as the economy increasingly matured. This proceeded quite rapidly until the overwhelming majority of the people were settled in cities or their suburbs and only a handful was left to tend to the farms.

Hoselitz (1953) contends that cities can also play a catalytic role in the economic growth of less developed countries (LDCs). Jones (1972) maintains that urbanization is part and parcel of economic transformation which can be guided onto a socially desirable pattern.[1] In the same vein, Dotson and Teune (1972), taking the Philippines as a case, suggest that urbanization should not be stopped but managed since it is not a negative but a positive force for national development. Friedmann (1968) even advocates a policy of "deliberate" and accelerated urbanization in order to step up development. At the same time, urban centers are found to play an important role in the political development of emerging nations like the Philippines (Laquian, 1966).

The rapid pace at which LDCs are imagined to have been urbanizing after the war, however, has led to contrasting views. Many believe that urbanization is, to a large extent, not the result of economic development (Weitz, 1973). They say that the conditions of poverty and rapid population growth in rural areas push massive numbers of people to the cities only to exacerbate the problems of urban unemployment and crowding (Myrdal, 1968:470). Thus, urbanization has far overtaken socioeconomic development, giving rise to "overurbanization" or "pseudourbanization" (McGee, 1967 and 1971).

In the preceding chapters, we have shown that rapid urbanization via massive rural-to-urban migration in the Philippines and probably in other LDCs is a misconception. The objective in this chapter is to demonstrate that urbanization was closely associated with economic development in the Philippines. It is maintained that sluggish urbanization in recent decades accompanied slow economic transformation, and that differential urbanization can be linked to differential development among regions and provinces.

We first view Philippine economic development in the context of Southeast and East Asian countries. Then we look into the performance of the country's different regions. To conclude, we analyze urbanization and socioeconomic development further in a regression framework using the cross-section of provinces as units of observation.

THE NATIONAL PERFORMANCE

Table 22 illustrates a strong association between stages of economic growth and urbanization in Southeast and East Asian countries. The correl

TABLE 22

Levels of GNP Per Capita and Urbanization
in Selected Asian Countries, 1970

Country	GNP Per Capita US$	Percent Urban	Percent City
Japan	1,920	82.2	56.3
Taiwan	390	64.4	37.6
Western Malaysia	380	45.3	17.1
South Korea	250	37.9	32.5
Philippines	210	32.9	16.7
Thailand	200	14.8	7.9
Indonesia	80	17.2	12.1
Burma	80	18.5	6.9

SOURCES: GNP per capita—International Bank for Reconstruction and Development (1972); percent urban—Table 9; and percent city—Table 10.

tion coefficient between GNP per capita and proportion of urban population is 0.83, and that between GNP per capita and proportion of city population is 0.84. The rank order is almost impeccable, especially for economic
level above $200 per capita and urbanization above 30 percent.

Table 23 shows the shift of labor force to the nonprimary or industrial
sector away from agriculture in selected Asian countries during the 1950s
and 1960s. The rate of sectoral shift in total labor force for the Philippines
was comparable to that of Western Malaysia and close to the rates of the
more advanced countries, viz. South Korea and Japan. A sex breakdown,
however, reveals that it was the nonprimary share of female labor force
that manifested a sharp increase (from 31 to 65 percent) in the 1950s,
while that of the males dropped from 36 to 31 percent, although it rose
again to 39 percent by 1970.[2] In none of the other countries was there
a similar downward shift for male and sharp upward shift for female labor
force share in the urban sector.

Table 24 presents the shares of gross domestic product (GDP) originating
in the nonprimary sector for the same group of Asian countries during
the 1960s. Only the Philippines and Burma exhibited falling industrial
product shares, even in the later half of the decade. Excepting the two
extremes of Japan and Indonesia, a striking similarity in the nonprimary
product shares of around 70 percent towards 1970 among the different
countries is apparent. This suggests that, unlike labor, the sectoral distribution of product may be loosely associated with rural-urban population
distribution.[3]

Further evidence of the sluggish transformation of the Philippine economy may be gleaned from comparative indices (United Nations, 1973a:
Table 23) on employment growth in manufacturing in the 1960s, as follows:

	1963	1967	1970
Philippines	100	105	109
Western Malaysia	100	126	—
South Korea	100	175	216
Japan	100	111	120

While manufacturing employment in the Philippines expanded by only
9 percent in seven years, in South Korea and Japan the rates were 116 and
20 percent, respectively. Likewise, in only four years Western Malaysia
generated a 26 percent increase in manufacturing employment.

TABLE 23

Proportion of Economically Active Population in Nonprimary Activities[1]
in Selected Asian Countries (in percent)

Country / Year	Total	Annual Percent Change	Male	Annual Percent Change	Female	Annual Percent Change
Philippines						
1948*	34.3		36.4		31.1	
1960	39.5	1.2	30.8	-1.4	65.0	6.3
1970	48.5	2.1	39.0	2.4	68.6	0.6
Thailand						
1947*	15.2		18.3		11.8	
1960	18.1	1.4	22.0	1.4	14.0	1.3
Western Malaysia						
1957	42.5		48.4		24.3	
1967-68*	50.9	1.7				
Indonesia						
1961	32.0		30.5		35.8	
1964-65*	32.8	0.7	30.9	0.4	36.5	0.6
South Korea						
1960	38.1		39.7		34.1	
1971*	53.4	3.1	57.4	3.4	46.4	2.8
Japan						
1955	59.0		66.3		47.5	
1960	67.4	2.7	74.2	2.3	56.9	3.7
1970*	80.9	1.8	85.3	1.4	74.1	2.7

1. Nonprimary activities exclude agriculture, forestry, hunting, and fishing.
SOURCES: Dates with asterisks—International Labor Office (1959:Table 4, and 1972:Table 2A); other years—United Nations (1964:Table 9); 1970 Philippines—NCSO, 1970 Census.

TABLE 24

Proportion of GDP from Nonprimary Activities[1]
in Selected Asian Countries (in percent)

Country Year	Nonprimary Product Share	Annual Percent Change
Philippines		
1960	73	
1965	75	0.5
1970	70	−1.4
Thailand		
1960	60	
1965	65	1.6
1969	68	1.1
Western Malaysia		
1960	66	
1965	73	2.0
1967	74	0.7
Indonesia		
1960	46	
1965	41	−2.3
1970	52	4.9
Burma		
1962	69	
1965	68	−0.5
1967	66	−1.5
South Korea		
1960	63	
1965	61	−0.7
1970	72	3.4
Japan		
1960	87	
1965	90	0.7
1970	93	0.7

1. Nonprimary activities exclude agriculture, forestry, hunting, and fishing.
SOURCE: United Nations (1973b: Table 3).

It is ironic that the performance of the industrial sector in the Philippines was discernibly weak, despite the fact that economic policy in the 1950s and early 1960s was profoundly imbued with the concern for industrialization via import substitution (Myint, 1972; Sicat, 1972). Industry was lavishly favored to the extent of taking agriculture for granted. Worse yet, this industrialization strategy turned out to be inordinately capital-intensive, with the consequence that the urban-industrial sector could not generate the capacity to absorb migrant labor from the rural sector.[4]

On the side of the agricultural sector, data on cereal production of the five Southeast Asian countries reveal that, during the 1954-1963 period, the growth of population exceeded the increase in cereal output in the Philippines and Indonesia (Hicks and McNicoll, 1971:32). In Thailand, Burma, and Western Malaysia, the edge of output growth over population growth ranged from over one-fourth to just under two-thirds. Productivity was the lowest in the Philippines, contributing only 13 percent to output change, with the remainder accounted for by expansion in farm area.[5] Stagnant agricultural productivity meant that farm workers had to keep increasing their numbers *pari passu* with the expansion of farmlands to be able to furnish, if barely, the necessary crops to a fast-growing population.[6] This is evidenced in Table 25 which shows labor and land productivities as well as land/labor ratio in the Philippines from 1950 to 1968.

TABLE 25

Philippines: Agricultural Indices, 1950-1968
(1955 = 100)

Year	Output/Labor	Output/Land	Land/Labor
1950	86	91	94
1955	100	100	100
1960	103	96	108
1965	112	105	107
1968	102	106	96

SOURCE: Hicks and McNicoll (1971:57).

Finally, a slackening in aggregate economic growth after 1950 can also be pointed out. While there are no data on GNP before the war, the average annual growth rates of real GNP and GNP per capita appear to have decelerated steadily from the 1946-1950 period to the subsequent two decades. This decrease can be seen in Table 26. The tempo of urbanization gives some indication of a pickup during the 1960s, although the GNP growth rates continued their slowdown.

In sum, the relative slowness of Philippine urbanization in the 1950s and 1960s was closely associated with the weakness of economic transformation and overall economic growth. On the one hand, with agricultural technology stagnant, there was constant need for more and more laborers to put new land frontiers to agricultural use. On the other hand, the demand for migrant labor in the urban sector was inadequate (except perhaps in the service subsector) because industrialization was of the labor-saving type. Of course, this is not to say that rural-to-urban migration was slight and of manageable proportions. The flow of migrant labor into Metro Manila, for example, has been huge, compounding the unemployment problem. But the whole point is that a wholesome development in both agriculture and industry might have allowed even more rural-urban migration, and thus faster urbanization.[7] Putting it differently, the conditions in both agriculture and industry were less conducive to intersectoral migration than otherwise, i.e., there was less pressure from the rural areas, and cities were not that attractive.[8]

REGIONAL DEVELOPMENT

The data on urbanization at the regional level showed that the more urbanized regions were also the ones that urbanized relatively rapidly, excepting Metro Manila, of course. Between 1939 and 1960, these regions exhibited an average urbanization tempo of 2.6 percent annually in contrast to 1.0 percent for the less urbanized group and 0.8 percent for the frontier regions. During 1960-1970, the urbanization tempos were 1.9, 0.4, and –0.2 percent, respectively. By 1970, the more urbanized group was 30.5 per urban, while the other two groups virtually stagnated at between 18 and 20 percent. This difference is a very significant one, indeed. It took approximately thirty-one years for the country as a whole to transform itself from 19 percent to 30 percent urban. Underlying the

TABLE 26

Philippines: Urbanization Levels, Real GNP,[1] and
Annual Rates of Growth

Year	Urbanization (percent)	Annual Tempo (percent)	Aggregate GNP (P millions)	Annual Change (percent)	Per Capita GNP (P)	Annual Change (percent)
1939[2]	21.6		5,272		293	
1950	27.5	2.9	10,008	17.4	494	13.9
1960	29.8	1.2	18,782	6.5	685	3.3
1970	32.9	1.5	31,747	5.4	861	2.3

1. At constant 1967 market prices.
2. 1946 for GNP.
SOURCES: Urbanization—Table 1; GNP—National Economic and Development Authority (NEDA).

TABLE 27

Regional Fertility and Mortality Indicators, ca. 1970

Region	Fertility			Mortality[2]		
	CBR	TFR	SMAM	CDR	e_0^0	IMR
More Urbanized	39.5	5.56^1	23.9^1	8.14	62.3^1	60.3^1
Manila and Southern Luzon	40.3	5.02	24.2	7.67	62.2	60.4
Central Luzon	37.6	5.75	24.4	7.64	64.6	50.3
Western Visayas	40.4	5.91	23.1	9.94	60.0	70.2
Less Urbanized	40.5	6.03^1	23.3^1	9.00	61.6^1	63.3^1
Ilocos	35.8	5.52	22.6	9.39	61.4	64.1
Bicol	40.0	6.25	24.6	6.76	64.3	51.6
Eastern and Central Visayas	42.2	6.33	22.7	10.11	59.2	74.3
Frontier	49.2	6.57^1	21.2^1	9.54	58.6^1	80.8^1
Cagayan	38.9	5.98	20.1	10.24	57.5	81.9
Mindanao	51.4	7.16	22.4	9.39	59.8	79.6
Philippines	42.3	5.89	23.7	9.17	60.6	67.6

1. Unweighted average.
2. The mortality measures were derived using the Brass technique. The CDRs and IMRs are somewhat underestimated, and the e_0^0's somewhat overestimated, but the relative differentials between regions, especially the broad regional groupings, are reasonably indicative. The more realistic estimates for the national level are: CDR = 11-12, e_0^0 = 58, and IMR = 70.

SOURCES: CBR & CDR—NCSO, 1970 Census; TFR—Concepcion (1974: Table 3) from 1973 NDS; SMAM—Smith (1974a:Table A) from 1973 NDS; other mortality indicators—Zablan (1975:Table 1) from 1973 NDS.

pronounced dissimilarities in urbanization have been differences in fertility, mortality, and net migration across regions and between sectors within regions. Demographic differentials, no doubt, also reflect variations in socioeconomic development.

Differences in fertility indicators across regions are given in Table 27. The more urbanized regions generally had lower crude birth rates (CBR) and lower total fertility rates (TFR), along with later singulate mean ages at marriage (SMAM), compared to the less urbanized and frontier regions. The differences between the more urbanized group and the frontier group are particularly clear: about ten births per thousand population, one child per woman, and 2.7 years for age at marriage. Associated mortality differences are also evident in Table 27. The least urbanized or the frontier regions evinced the highest crude death rates (CDR), the shortest life expectancies at birth (e_o^o), and the highest infant mortality rates (IMR). Conversely, the more urbanized regions were the most favored with respect to mortality.

Estimates of fertility and mortality differences between rural and urban sectors for each region are not available. Nonetheless, overall estimates from the 1973 NDS clearly suggest measurable intersectoral differences in vital rates, as follows:

	CBR	CDR
Metropolitan	36.3	6.6
Other Urban	35.1	9.4
Rural	44.8	11.1
National	41.9	10.6

The CBRs are plausible; the CDRs are somewhat on the low side, yet the relative intersectoral differences are reasonably indicative.

As we shall see in subsequent chapters, both the volume and quality of internal migration streams are patterned among regions and sectors according to their urbanization levels. That is, the more urbanized the region, the greater volume of positively selected urban in-migrants. This process tends to accentuate interregional disparities in economic development as reflected in industrialization and income levels.

Table 28 shows that in 1960 about two-fifths of the labor force in the more urbanized regions were employed in the industrial sector, compared to less than one-third in the less urbanized regions. In 1970, the disparity widened to 24 percentage points as more than one-half (56 percent) of the labor force was industrialized in the more urbanized regions and only one-third in the less urbanized group. On the other hand, there was a nine-point difference between the less urbanized and frontier regions in 1960, which narrowed to merely four points in 1970. With the extreme levels of Manila City excluded, the correlation coefficient (r) between levels of urbanization and industrialization for the eleven regions was

TABLE 28

Regional Urbanization and Labor Force Industrialization Levels,
1960 and 1970 (in percent)

Region	1960		1970	
	URB[1]	IND[2]	URB[1]	IND[2]
Manila	100.0	98.9	100.0	98.6
More Urbanized	33.8	40.7	40.2	55.8
Central Luzon	28.0	41.6	33.8	60.2
Southern Luzon	47.9	52.5	56.6	67.5
Western Visayas	30.5	30.6	27.6	41.7
Central Visayas	22.2	33.7	28.5	41.5
Less Urbanized	19.8	27.1	20.5	32.2
Ilocos	17.6	19.9	20.6	31.7
Bicol	21.9	31.6	21.8	36.4
Eastern Visayas	18.9	28.6	19.0	27.9
Frontier	18.6	18.2	18.3	28.3
Cagayan	14.1	13.6	14.3	22.4
Western Mindanao	16.8	18.9	16.2	24.9
Northern Mindanao	20.2	22.9	18.7	34.5
Southern Mindanao	20.9	15.4	21.5	27.6
Philippines	29.8	34.1	32.9	45.4

1. URB refers to level of urbanization. Figures for the more urbanized group, Central Luzon and Southern Luzon, are different from those in other tables because of the inclusion of municipalities that should be in Metro Manila; the adjustments were necessary for correspondence with the labor force data.

2. IND refers to industrialization of employed workers aged 10 and over, i.e., proportion of labor in nonprimary activities.

SOURCES: Table 5, and Domingo and Zosa (1975:Table 3) from censuses.

0.87 for 1960 and 0.93 for 1970. Moreover, a positive, though weak ($r = 0.25$), relationship obtained between tempos of urbanization and industrialization during the interval.[9]

A close positive association is also evident between regional urbanization and family income levels in Table 29. The correlation coefficient is

TABLE 29

Regional Urbanization and Mean Family Income Levels,
ca. 1970

Region	1970 Urbanization (percent)	1971 Mean Family Income (₱ annum)
Greater Manila[1]	100.0	7,785
More Urbanized	34.9	3,943
Central Luzon	33.8	4,127
Southern Luzon	41.1	4,332
Western Visayas	27.6	3,206
Less Urbanized	22.9	2,754
Ilocos	20.6	3,299
Bicol	21.8	2,785
Eastern and Central Visayas	24.3	2,548
Frontier	18.3	3,217
Cagayan	14.3	2,390
Northern and Western Mindanao	17.7	3,062
Southern Mindanao	21.5	3,577
Philippines	32.9	3,736

1. Greater Manila is a smaller version of Metro Manila and comprises the cities of Manila, Quezon, Caloocan, and Pasay, and the municipalities of Makati, Mandaluyong, San Juan, and Navotas. Adjustments in urbanization levels for the other regions were also necessary for conformity with family income data.

SOURCES: Table 5, and NCSO (1972c:Table 1).

0.78 with Greater Manila excluded and goes up to 0.97 with the inclusion of Greater Manila.[10] It is interesting that the frontier regions generally had higher incomes compared to the less urbanized regions. Although the frontier regions appeared to be disadvantaged in terms of the vital processes (fertility and mortality) and industrialization, as noted above, they seemed to be better off with respect to income because of their agricultural endowments. For this reason, whereas the less urbanized regions suffered severe out-migration, the frontier regions experienced substantial in-migration and comparatively little out-migration.

PROVINCE-LEVEL ANALYSIS

Thus far, we have put together some evidence on the link of urbanization with development at the national and regional levels. In this section, we attempt to subject the hypothesized relationship to a more rigorous test in a regression framework. The causal relationship is most likely two-way, but here we are concerned with the influence of development on urbanization. Although it may seem logical to assume that this influence exists, two things remain to be investigated, namely: (1) the specific development variables involved, and (2) the relative importance these variables assume. For this type of analysis, we do not have national or regional data over a sufficiently long time series. Hence, we resort to a cross-sectional approach using province-level data.[11] Descending to less aggregative data may, in fact, help deepen the analysis.

Theoretical Model

The general model to be tested may be formulated as

$$U = f(MC, FM, R, CWR, UI, FD, RN, PM, e)$$

where

U = level of urbanization or proportion urban,

MC = manufacturing and commercial establishments (employing ten or more workers) per 100,000 population,

FM = farm machines (tractors and harvesting machines) per 100,000 farm population,

R = radio ownership—percent of occupied dwelling units with radio,

CWR = child-woman ratio—children aged five to nine per 1,000 women aged twenty to forty-nine,

UI   =   urban-rural in-migration ratio—the ratio of the
         number of urban in-migrants to rural in-migrants
         in a province from other provinces,

FD   =   farm density—farm population per 1,000 hectares
         of farm area,

RN   =   road network—kilometers of roads (weighted by
         type) per 1,000 kilometers of land area, and

PM   =   proximity to Metro Manila—a dummy variable taking
         the value of 1 if a province belongs to the region
         of Central Luzon or Southern Luzon and 0 other-
         wise.

The independent variables may be roughly classified as: economic—
MC and FM; social variable—R; demographic variables—CWR, UI, and
FD; and situational variables—RN and PM. MC denotes the degree of
provincial industrialization and commercialization. Inasmuch as industrial
and commercial establishments are mostly located in urban areas, they
would exert a "pull" from rural areas. FM indicates the level of farm
mechanization or the state of agricultural technology, which would tend
to displace actual as well as potential farmworkers, who would then be
inclined to migrate to urban areas. R signifies several things, such as levels
of both intra- and interprovincial communication, literacy, and relative
affluence—all of which would have a positive impact on urbanization.
CWR is a proxy for level of fertility and burden of dependency, which
would have a retardative effect on migration and urbanization. Alternatively, to the extent that rural fertility is higher than urban fertility, it
could exert a demographic pressure to migrate from rural areas. UI is designed to capture the exogenous impact of in-migration in urban areas
relative to in-migration in rural areas of a province from other provinces.
FD is assumed to measure the "push" from the farms, which would mean
a positive effect on urbanization. RN would also exert a positive effect
on urbanization to the extent that it facilitates, or lowers the barriers to,
spatial mobility. Finally, PM is a measure of the radial influence of Metropolitan Manila on surrounding provinces relative to other provinces located
farther away.

We assume that the effects on urbanization of socioeconomic and
demographic conditions at a particular period would materialize only

after some time lag. In other words, a "lagged effects" model would explain differences in provincial levels of urbanization at time $t+n$ using the independent variables at time t. Alternatively, we may assume that conditions at the start of some time interval affect changes in urbanization levels during the interval. Accordingly, a "deviational changes"[12] model would use the independent variables at time t to explain changes in provincial levels of urbanization between t and $t+n$.

Hence, the general model may be specified as two types of equations. The lagged effects equation would be stated as

$$U_{t+n} = f(MC_t, FM_t, R_t, CWR_t, UI_{t+n-t}, FD_t, RN_t, PM).$$

The deviational changes equation would be formulated as

$$U_{t+n} - \hat{U}_{t+n} = f(MC_t, FM_t, R_t, CWR_t, UI_{t+n-t}, FD_t, RN_t, PM)$$

where $\hat{U}_{t+n} = a + b\, U_t + e$, and the other notations are as defined above. To the extent that the independent variables in the two models are lagged, they are predetermined or exogenous. Consequently, they are independent of the error terms, and the problem of "simultaneous equations bias" is avoided.[13] As formulated, the models may be useful in predicting urbanization levels, say ten years hence, given the data on the explanatory variables now.

Empirical Results

The regression models are tested with the most recent data on urbanization and socioeconomic-demographic development at the provincial level, 1960-1970. Before going into regressions, an inspection of the correlation matrix of the variables to be used in the regressions would be instructive (Table 30). The matrix shows correlation signs in the expected direction between level of urbanization and all the explanatory variables. The expected signs also obtain between "deviational change" in urbanization level and the independent variables, except farm machineries. Furthermore, Table 30 reveals high correlations between only a few independent variables, namely, farm density and child-woman ratio (−0.63), and between metro proximity and radio ownership (0.66). To avoid multicollinearity, two highly correlated independent variables are not both used in the same regression run.

Table 31 displays the empirical results of the lagged effects model: regressions of 1970 provincial urbanization levels against 1960 develop-

TABLE 30

Correlation Matrix of Variables Used in Regressions

	1 MC	2 FM	3 R	4 CWR	5 UI	6 FD	7 RN	8 PM	9 U	10 U-U
1. Manufacturing & Commercial Establishments (MC)	1.000									
2. Farm Machineries (FM)	0.184	1.000								
3. Radio Ownership (R)	0.494	0.322	1.000							
4. Child-Woman Ratio (CWR)	-0.079	0.121	-0.160	1.000						
5. Urban-Rural In-Migration Ratio (UI)	0.323	0.120	0.413	-0.367	1.000					
6. Farm Density (FD)	0.231	-0.142	0.199	-0.632	0.226	1.000				
7. Road Network (RN)	0.066	0.057	0.328	-0.297	0.133	0.530	1.000			
8. Metro Proximity (PM)	0.114	0.232	0.660	-0.084	0.175	-0.029	0.168	1.000		
9. Urbanization Level (U)	0.579	0.419	0.792	-0.139	0.610	0.115	0.095	0.436	1.000	
10. Change in Urbanization Level (U-U)	0.441	-0.031	0.513	-0.327	0.463	0.264	0.197	0.335	0.539	1.000
Mean	8.453	65.092	6.809	936.346	0.626	1,880.935	139.633	0.283	21.847	0.032
Standard Deviation	6.254	102.289	5.411	85.373	0.736	801.547	79.979	0.450	12.339	6.745

Note: The basic data used for the correlation and regressions are given in the Appendix.

TABLE 31

The Lagged Effects Model: Regressions of 1970 Provincial
Urbanization Levels on 1960 Development Variables

Variable	Regression 1	Regression 2	Regression 3	Regression 4
Constant (a)	6.045	8.230	8.757	8.225
1. Manufacturing & Commercial Establishments, (MC)	0.341 (2.264)*	0.733 (4.085)**	0.342 (2.292)*	0.733 (4.248)**
2. Farm Machineries (FM)	0.021 (2.441)**	0.029 (2.702)**	0.021 (2.556)**	0.029 (2.812)**
3. Radio Ownership (R)	1.299 (6.606)**		1.300 (6.675)**	
4. Child-Woman Ratio (CWR)	0.003 (0.256)		—	
5. Urban/Rural In-migration (UI)	5.459 (4.216)**	7.039 (4.669)**	5.343 (4.448)**	7.038 (4.780)**
6. Farm Density (FD)		−0.000 (−0.003)		—
7. Road Network (RN)	−0.023 (−2.092)*	−0.007 (−0.443)	−0.024 (−2.269)*	−0.007 (−0.540)
8. Metro Proximity (PM)		7.434 (3.091)**		7.435 (3.157)**
R^2	0.805	0.686	0.804	0.686
$\overline{R}^2$	0.779	0.645	0.784	0.652
F-ratio	31.605**	16.733**	38.683**	20.516**

Note: The number of observations (provinces) is fifty-three, with Manila City and Rizal
province, which are too atypical, excluded. Figures in parentheses are the t-values; those
with two asterisks are significant at 1 percent level; and those with one asterisk are significant at 5 percent level.

ment indicators. Different regressions are necessary so that two highly correlated explanatory variables can be run separately. Thus, regression 1 has radio ownership and child-woman ratio instead of metro proximity and farm density, respectively, which in turn are included in regression 2. The results of regression 1 seem to be superior: all the regression coefficients, except one (child-woman ratio) are significant at least at the 5 percent level, and together they explain about 80 percent of the interprovincial variation in urbanization levels. Regression 2 gives two insignificant independent variables (farm density and road network) and a lower coefficient of determination (R^2) of 0.69. Regressions 3 and 4 show that dropping nonsignificant independent variables (child-woman ratio from regression 1 and farm density from regression 2, respectively) slightly enhances the significance of the remaining variables, and yet their combined explanatory power (R^2) remains stable for both regressions.

On the basis of the regressions using the lagged effects model, important determinants of provincial urbanization seem to be industrialization and commercialization, farm technology, better communication or higher literacy, urban in-migration from other provinces, and proximity to the metropolitan area. Child-woman ratio, a proxy for fertility and dependency burden, exhibits the positive sign but is insignificant. Farm density, an indicator of the rural demographic pressure to migrate, has the reverse sign and is also insignificant. It is curious that, contrary to our original expectation, road network has a moderate negative influence on urbanization. It may be that, instead of inducing one-way and permanent migrations, a good road system rather facilitates streams and counterstreams as well as short visits to urban centers and back to the countryside.

Table 32 gives the results of the deviational changes model: regressions of derived 1960-1970 urbanization level changes on 1960 development variables. With the exception of farm mechanization, which also exhibits the reverse sign, the same independent variables are significant, although the degree of significance is generally lower than in the previous model. The coefficients of determination (0.44 and 0.42) are likewise markedly lower than previously. Discarding the least significant predictors (regressions 3 and 4) results in slightly more significant coefficients and the same explanatory power (R^2) for the model.[14] On balance, the deviational changes model, though of inferior empirical results, corroborates the findings from the lagged effects model as to the chief determinants of urbanization.

TABLE 32

The Deviational Changes Model: Regressions of 1960-1970
Urbanization Level Changes on 1960 Development Variables

Variable	Regression 1	Regression 2	Regression 3	Regression 4
Constant (a)	4.840	−6.960	4.310	−6.934
1. Manufacturing & Commercial Establishments, (MC)	0.247 (1.742)*	0.363 (2.680)**	0.249 (1.777)*	0.362 (2.708)**
2. Farm Machineries (FM)	−0.013 (−1.596)	−0.012 (−1.456)	−0.013 (−1.613)*	−0.012 (−1.475)
3. Radio Ownership (R)	0.454 (2.439)**		0.443 (2.557)**	
4. Child-Woman Ratio (CWR)	−0.011 (−1.074)		−0.011 (−1.073)	
5. Urban/Rural Inmigration (UI)	2.037 (1.666)*	2.880 (2.545)**	2.045 (1.691)*	2.882 (2.575)**
6. Farm Density (FD)		0.001 (0.595)		0.001 (0.794)
7. Road Network (RN)	−0.002 (−0.172)	−0.001 (−0.094)	−	−
8. Metro Proximity (PM)		4.364 (2.401)**		4.404 (2.518)**
R^2	0.438	0.423	0.437	0.423
$\overline{R}^2$	0.363	0.346	0.376	0.360
F-ratio	5.837**	5.493**	7.150**	6.735**

Note: The number of observations (provinces) is fifty-two with the exclusion of Manila City and Rizal province which are too atypical, and Batanes province which was completely rural in both 1960 and 1970. Figures in parentheses are the t-values; those with two asterisks are significant at 1 percent level, and those with one asterisk are significant at 5 percent level.

SUMMARY AND CONCLUSION

In this chapter we have demonstrated the close positive relationship of urbanization to development. This relationship was borne out at the national, regional, and provincial levels. The slow pace of national urbanization in the 1950s and 1960s appears to have come hand in hand with sluggish economic growth and sectoral changes. An analysis at the regional level has also shown that the more urbanized regions were the more advanced in terms of demographic development (lower fertility and mortality), labor force industrialization, and income levels. Finally, multiple regression analyses of provincial data have further demonstrated that development variables were the main determinants of urbanization. Development variables that seem to ably predict urbanization were industrialization and commercialization, farm mechanization, better communication or higher literacy, urban in-migration from other provinces, and proximity to the metropolitan area. Demographic variables (child-woman ratio and farm density) denoting the rural pressure to migrate were insignificant.[15] Rather than induce permanent migration, better transportation seemed merely to improve rural-urban interchange. This is an apparently favorable implication for rural development.

NOTES

1. Analyzing cross-sectional data on about seventy-five countries, Schnore (1961) also concludes that urbanization is an intrinsic component of modernization in general.

2. An analysis of the occupational characteristics of rural-to-urban migrants from the 1973 National Demographic Survey data discloses that a good part of female migrants land in the service subsector, which is at best a soft yardstick of industrialization.

3. But this may be because primary production is largely of the subsistence, nonmonetized type, which means that it was probably not properly represented in GDP. Hence, its surprisingly tiny share in LDCs. Data for the Philippines in 1970, for example, suggest that three-fifths of the male labor force in agriculture contributed less than a third to aggregate output.

4. In the words of the chief economist: "The incentive pattern accelerated the establishment of industries which required more capital-intensity to the neglect of sectors which were also more dependent on the economy's resource base and those

industries which, relatively, depended more on labor-use, like cottage industries with excellent export potentials" (Sicat, 1972:267).

5. Malaysia, a rapidly urbanizing country as we have seen earlier, evinced the highest agricultural productivity hand in hand with the strongest industrial performance in the region.

6. While there may still be some unused gross potential of agricultural lands, it is dubious if land expansion can still be counted upon in the future, considering the cost of conversion and problems of ecological balance (ILO, 1974:82-83). See also pp. 55-108 on the need to mobilize the lethargic rural sector.

7. It is quite likely that, with sufficient development in both sectors, the rate of population growth might have been slower. As a result, although rural-urban migration might have been larger proportionately, it could have been smaller in absolute numbers.

8. Todaro (1969), for example, argues that the probability of migrating varies directly to the chance of landing a job in the city, allowing for a period of waiting.

9. Analogous to urbanization tempo, industrialization tempo is the difference between the growth rates of nonprimary and primary employed labor force.

10. A weak negative correlation is apparent between urbanization levels and intraregional income inequalities (Gini ratios).

11. The regions of the country are further subdivided into provinces. In 1960, there were fifty-four provinces excluding Greater Manila; in 1970, the number increased to sixty-six because some provinces were split. For the analysis, we use the fifty-three provinces of 1960 (less Rizal which is too atypical) because we have complete data for these.

12. This specification seems superior to absolute changes or the usual rates of change during an interval which would tend to be biased in favor of those at lower or higher levels. See Duncan, et al. (1961:162-163).

13. This would have been a problem as we could also assume an interactive relationship between urbanization and economic-demographic development. The only independent variable that appears simultaneous with the dependent variable is the urban/rural in-migration ratio (UI_{t+n-t}) in the deviational changes model, but this is assumed *a priori* as exogenous. On simultaneity bias, see, e.g., Johnston (1963:341 ff.) or Wonnacott and Wonnacott (1970:152 ff.). Greenwood (1975) elaborates on the simultaneity bias in single-equation, multiple-regression migration models.

14. We tried logarithmic transformations of the data for the two regression models, but the results were significantly inferior.

15. Several other studies show that the "push" factors are less important than the "pull" or development factors in migration and urbanization. See, e.g., Kumur (1973), Simkins and Wernstedt (1971), and Zachariah and Pernia (1975).

PATTERNS
OF INTERNAL
MIGRATION

5

The interregional patterns of internal migration in the Philippines were first presented by Simkins and Wernstedt (1963) for the period 1948-1960 using data from the 1960 Census. Subsequently, Pascual (1966) examined lifetime migration in the context of the ten regions (the old regional divisions) availing of place-of-birth and current-residence data also from the 1960 Census. She noted the principal regions of origin (Ilocos and Visayan regions) and of destination (Manila City, Southern Luzon, and Mindanao regions). Because migration data were collected for the first time only in 1960, an earlier analysis of migration for the period 1939-1948 had to resort to the census survival ratio method (Nava, 1959). This method, however, was also used by Kim (1972) in anticipation of the 1970 Census results.

Migration data at the provincial level (from the 1960 Census) were analyzed by Zosa (1973) in a multiple regression framework in order to identify the correlates of interprovincial migration. Smith (1974b), on the other hand, attempted to single out underlying patterns of interprovincial movements by means of factor analysis. Other researchers focused on in-migration in Mindanao (Vandermeer and Agaloos, 1961) or in particular areas in Mindanao (Simkins and Wernstedt, 1971; Ulack, 1972) and the Visayas (Hart, 1971).

A recent study of interregional migration was undertaken by Smith (1975a) using data from the 1970 Census. He compared patterns of migration during birth-1970 and 1960-1970 with those during birth-1960 and observed some important shifts. First, interprovincial lifetime mobility of the total population rose from 15.8 percent for 1960 to 17.6 percent for 1970; interregionally, mobility increased from 12.7 to 13.4 percent.[1] Second, the extent of long-distance movements was remarkable, although this seems to have tapered off somewhat: of the total of lifetime inter-provincial migrants in 1960, 82.7 percent had moved from one region to another, and in 1970 the proportion was 74.7 percent. Third, interregional streams during the 1960s were, on the whole, less effective (i.e., counter-streams or return flows became more consequential) compared to earlier streams. Fourth, sex ratios were generally high (i.e., male-dominance) for long-distance and rural- or frontier-destined migrations, but low for short-distance and urbanward movements; overall, women seem to have figured more prominently in recent migrations.

In Chapter 3, we examined the relative share of rural-urban migration in urban population growth, and we saw that it was generally minor vis-à-vis the natural increase and reclassification components. But regression analysis in Chapter 4 showed that the urban-rural in-migration ratio was one of the significant explanatory variables in differential urbanization among provinces. That is, provinces that were highly urbanized had ex-perienced relatively heavy urban in-migration. In this chapter, we concern ourselves with the broad patterns of internal migration as they relate to urbanization and development. We will address the following questions: (1) what are the principal migration streams and how does the rural-urban stream figure among them; (2) to what extent and in what way are the patterns of internal migration related to the regional patterns of urbaniza-tion and development; (3) given that the majority of internal migrants travel long distances and cross regional borders, as pointed out above, does migration also mean for them significant changes in socioeconomic milieu; (4) do the interregional differences in levels of urbanization and development signify that the metropolitan and more urbanized regions are the principal destinations, and the less urbanized and frontier regions the origins of migrants; and (5) what are the major migration interchanges?

For the analysis, we utilize mainly the 1960 Census data on place of birth and current residence as well as the 1970 Census data on place of residence in 1960 and current residence.[2] The purpose is to detect impor-tant shifts in recent period migration vis-à-vis previous lifetime migration. We supplement census data with information from the 1973 NDS which can be presented by rural-urban origins and destinations.[3]

TABLE 33

Regional Lifetime Migration Rates,
1960 and 1970 (per thousand)

Region	In-Migration		Out-Migration		Net Migration	
	1960	1970	1960	1970	1960	1970
Manila City	442.5	392.2	331.6	359.6	180.9	52.4
More Urbanized	83.7	107.8	139.3	141.7	−62.6	−38.8
Central Luzon	40.9	58.0	138.1	136.3	−119.4	−86.7
Southern Luzon	193.4	211.3	47.1	44.7	166.3	191.1
Western Visayas	22.7	29.3	142.5	164.2	−130.6	−149.4
Central Visayas	31.3	46.2	243.1	267.2	−245.5	−262.1
Less Urbanized	29.8	42.0	118.2	157.6	−95.4	−128.4
Ilocos	39.1	48.6	154.6	193.0	−127.9	−164.2
Bicol	34.7	45.5	83.6	116.9	−51.9	−77.7
Eastern Visayas	18.1	33.2	131.7	180.2	−122.8	−164.5
Frontier	248.1	216.4	69.3	57.7	212.5	183.9
Cagayan	135.6	126.6	56.3	62.8	87.7	70.4
Western Mindanao	292.4	189.4	37.3	49.6	305.5	158.9
Northern Mindanao	166.3	176.0	118.2	76.2	56.0	114.2
Southern Mindanao	376.7	321.6	27.6	36.9	437.5	346.9
Philippines	127.4	134.2	127.4	134.2	0	0

Note: In-migration rate = in-migration as a proportion of enumerated population. Out-migration rate = out-migration as a proportion of population born in a region, i.e., enumerated population plus out-migration minus in-migration. Net migration rate = net migration as a proportion of the average of the base populations for the in-migration and out-migration rates. (See U.N. Manual VI, pp. 41-42).

SOURCE: Annex, Table C; and NCSO, 1960 and 1970 censuses.

REGIONAL IN- AND OUT-MIGRATION

The regional patterns of lifetime in- and out-migration rates for 1960 and 1970 are shown in Table 33 (based on the absolute numbers of migrants in the Annex for Chapter 5, Table C). Three observations from the table should be emphasized here. First, there was a general shift from frontierward to metro-oriented movement; this meant a tapering of in-migration rates to Cagayan and Mindanao regions (as well as to Manila City) and a corresponding inflation of the in-migration rate to Southern Luzon which contains the metropolitan area. Second, the less urbanized regions of Ilocos, Bicol, and Eastern Visayas continued to be heavy net out-migration areas with the said reorientation from frontier to metro-politan destination. Third, the more urbanized regions were not homo-geneous, for three (Central Luzon, Western Visayas, and Central Visayas) suffered net out-movements. The net loss for the more urbanized group was mild, however, compared to that for the less urbanized regions for both 1960 and 1970.

Regional migration rates for the period 1960-1970 are shown in Table 34 (based on absolute numbers in the Annex, Table D). Here, the varia-tions across regions are even clearer. Manila City suffered a net outflow, denoting the trend toward suburbanization. The more urbanized group experienced a net inflow as a result of the huge gain for the metropolitan region in Southern Luzon. The less urbanized regions, as expected, all suf-fered net losses. The frontier regions all evinced net gains.

BROAD INTERREGIONAL STREAMS

One way of relating interregional migration streams to the regional pattern of urbanization and development is to cast them in the metro-politan, more urbanized, less urbanized, and frontier regions framework.[4] This simple framework collapses the huge 12 x 12 interregional matrix into a more manageable 4 x 4 matrix and yet enhances its analytic power, at least for our purposes. The regions are grouped not according to their geographic contiguity but according to their urbanization and develop-ment characteristics as determined in earlier chapters (see map in Chapter 2). The matrix allows us to identify the major flows of people that entail not only physical or geographic mobility but also environmental and social changes.

Birth-1960 Migration

The total number of lifetime migrants (all ages) as of 1960 across all twelve regions was 3,523,373. Their distribution by broad regions of origin and destination is given in Table 35, which also includes migrants between individual regions within each broad region (i.e., the numbers in the diagonal), except for Metro Manila which is considered an individual region. Subtracting interregional migrants who remained within the broad regional groupings gives the total number of migrants who crossed broad regional borders or who transferred from one socioeconomic type of region to another. This number was about 3,043,000, or 86.4 percent of

TABLE 34

Regional Period Migration Rates, 1960-1970 (per thousand)

Region	In-Migration	Out-Migration	Net Migration
Manila City	193.4	416.7	−223.3
More Urbanized	77.1	69.4	+7.7
Central Luzon	47.2	66.7	−19.5
Southern Luzon	151.4	33.2	+118.2
Western Visayas	22.5	83.3	−60.8
Central Visayas	38.5	130.7	−92.2
Less Urbanized	34.4	87.3	−52.9
Ilocos	38.3	93.8	−55.5
Bicol	37.0	67.5	−30.5
Eastern Visayas	28.5	106.7	−78.2
Frontier	103.9	44.2	+59.7
Cagayan	56.6	41.0	+15.6
Western Mindanao	76.6	45.5	+31.1
Northern Mindanao	106.9	49.2	+57.7
Southern Mindanao	145.7	40.0	+105.7
Philippines	80.0	80.0	0.0

Note: The base population is the average population during the decade.
SOURCE: Annex, Table D; and NCSO, 1960 and 1970 censuses.

TABLE 35

Birth-1960 Migration by Broad Regions of Origin and Destination

Region of Birth	Region of Residence, 1960				
	Metro Manila	More Urbanized	Less Urbanized	Frontier	Total
Metro Manila		84,722	21,424	22,933	129,079
More Urbanized	840,371	210,603	113,900	1,118,321	2,283,195
Less Urbanized	322,900	167,738	14,490	237,241	742,369
Frontier	53,437	39,297	20,720	255,276	368,730
Total	1,216,708	502,360	170,534	1,633,771	3,523,373

Note: The matrix includes persons of all ages who moved between the broad regional groupings as well as those who moved between individual regions under the broad regional groupings. The complete matrix that includes the nonmigrants can be referred to in the Annex, Table E.

Metro Manila comprises Manila City and Rizal province, an approximation of the formally accepted Metro Manila definition.

SOURCE: NCSO, 1960 Census.

all interregional migrants—indeed, a very appreciable proportion. Table 35 also shows that, in terms of absolute volume, the largest streams were from the more urbanized to the frontier regions and to Metro Manila, and the smallest streams were those within the less urbanized group and from the frontier and metro regions to the less urbanized regions.

Lifetime migrants at each destination (1960 regions of residence) are distributed according to their respective origins (regions of birth) in Table 36. In other words, Table 36 answers the question: where do migrants at each destination come from? The more urbanized regions (MR) were by far the principal sources (roughly two-thirds on the average) of migrants for all four regions. In Metro Manila (MM) alone, 69 percent of migrants were born in MR. Likewise, the less urbanized (LR) and frontier (FR) groups drew approximately 67 percent of their migrants from the same source. Even migration between one region and another within the MR group was more dominant (42 percent) than migration into MR from any of the external sources.

Table 37 responds to the question: where do migrants from each origin go to? The pattern looks varied. Fully two-thirds of migrants born in MM were living in MR in 1960. Almost half the migrants born in MR were found in FR and more than a third in MM. Of those born in LR, 44 percent were found in MM and 32 percent in FR in 1960. The majority (69 percent) of those born in FR, however, merely moved between one frontier region and another. Thus, unlike the case in Table 36 where MR could be generalized as the chief source of lifetime migrants, Table 37 suggests that no single destination was favored by all streams. Each origin had its own favored destination.

The foregoing distributions of migration streams by origin and destination did not take into account population sizes at origin or destination. A measure of migration propensity that controls for sending and receiving populations is the index of preference or relative intensity.[5] This gives the ratio of the observed volume of a migration stream to what would be expected if the volume were determined by population size at origin and destination. Table 38 shows that migration streams from the more urbanized and less urbanized regions to both the metro and frontier regions, especially to the former, were of very high relative intensities. The actual streams from the more urbanized and less urbanized regions to the metro region, for example, were more than four times and nearly four times, respectively, what would be expected. Migration be-

TABLE 36

Birth-1960 Migration by Broad Regions of Destination
and Percent Distribution by Origin

Region of Birth	Region of Residence, 1960				
	Metro Manila	More Urbanized	Less Urbanized	Frontier	Total
Metro Manila		16.9	12.6	1.4	3.7
More Urbanized	69.1	41.9	66.8	68.4	64.8
Less Urbanized	26.5	33.4	8.5	14.5	21.1
Frontier	4.4	7.8	12.2	15.6	10.5
Total	100.0	100.0	100.0	100.0	100.0

TABLE 37

Birth-1960 Migration by Broad Regions of Origin
and Percent Distribution by Destination

Region of Birth	Region of Residence, 1960				
	Metro Manila	More Urbanized	Less Urbanized	Frontier	Total
Metro Manila		65.6	16.6	17.8	100.0
More Urbanized	36.8	9.2	5.0	49.0	100.0
Less Urbanized	43.5	22.6	2.0	32.0	100.0
Frontier	14.5	10.7	5.6	69.2	100.0
Total	34.5	14.3	4.8	46.4	100.0

TABLE 38

Index of Preference: Birth-1960 Migration by Broad Regions
of Origin and Destination (in percent)

Region of Birth	Region of Residence, 1960			
	Metro Manila	More Urbanized	Less Urbanized	Frontier
Metro Manila		87.7	44.2	44.3
More Urbanized	457.6	26.5	29.3	262.7
Less Urbanized	375.8	45.1	7.9	118.9
Frontier	77.2	13.1	14.4	160.2

tween frontier regions was also relatively intense. The index of preference was comparatively low for flows to the more urbanized and less urbanized regions.

1960-1970 Migration

Table 39 gives the number of interregional migrants (1,954,000 persons ten years of age and over in 1970) between 1960 and 1970 according to the major streams. Of these migrants, only 14.4 percent migrated within the same general environment. The vast majority (85.6 percent, about the same proportion as for lifetime migrants) did not only negotiate long distances but also surmounted socioeconomic barriers. With respect to volume, the streams from the more urbanized to the frontier and metro regions continued to stand out, while those between the less urbanized regions and from the frontier to the less urbanized group were still the smallest. The distributions of the migration flows according to where they originate and where they end up are portrayed in Tables 40 and 41, respectively.

Table 40 shows that the more urbanized regions were generally less important as origins of recent period migrations than they were of earlier lifetime migrations. They remained relatively important sources, however,

TABLE 39

1960-1970 Migration by Broad Regions of Origin and Destination

Region of Residence 1960	Region of Residence, 1970				
	Metro Manila	More Urbanized	Less Urbanized	Frontier	Total
Metro Manila		156,598	68,734	37,208	262,540
More Urbanized	352,593	125,121	64,471	386,601	928,786
Less Urbanized	232,910	124,588	10,881	107,742	476,121
Frontier	48,842	70,711	21,501	145,115	286,169
Total	634,345	477,018	165,587	676,666	1,953,616

Note: The matrix includes persons 10 years old and over by 1970 who moved between the broad regional groupings, as well as those who moved between individual regions under the broad regional groupings. The complete matrix that includes the non-migrants can be referred to in the Annex, Table F.

Metro Manila comprises Manila City and Rizal province, an approximation of the formally accepted Metro Manila definition.
SOURCE: NCSO, 1970 Census.

TABLE 40

1960-1970 Migration by Broad Regions of Destination
and Percent Distribution by Origin

Region of Residence 1960	Region of Residence, 1970				
	Metro Manila	More Urbanized	Less Urbanized	Frontier	Total
Metro Manila		32.8	41.5	5.5	13.4
More Urbanized	55.6	26.2	38.9	57.1	47.5
Less Urbanized	36.7	26.1	6.6	15.9	24.4
Frontier	7.7	14.8	13.0	21.4	14.6
Total	100.0	100.0	100.0	100.0	100.0

TABLE 41

1960-1970 Migration by Broad Regions of Origin and Percent Distribution by Destination

Region of Residence 1960	Region of Residence, 1970				
	Metro Manila	More Urbanized	Less Urbanized	Frontier	Total
Metro Manila		59.6	26.2	14.2	100.0
More Urbanized	38.0	13.5	6.9	41.6	100.0
Less Urbanized	48.9	26.2	2.3	22.6	100.0
Frontier	17.1	24.7	7.5	50.7	100.0
Total	32.5	24.4	8.5	34.6	100.0

TABLE 42

Index of Preference: 1960-1970 Migration by Broad Regions
of Origin and Destination (in percent)

Region of Residence 1960	Region of Residence, 1970			
	Metro Manila	More Urbanized	Less Urbanized	Frontier
Metro Manila		175.0	179.4	70.7
More Urbanized	330.8	32.1	38.3	170.4
Less Urbanized	497.5	73.2	15.0	108.3
Frontier	87.3	34.7	23.9	121.4

for streams to MM and to FR. MM became a prominent origin of flows
to MR and LR. LR increased its share to MM but decreased that to MR.
FR remained a minor source of out-migrants, but mobility between FR
regions increased.

The pattern of destinations for the 1960-1970 migration streams was
similar to that for lifetime streams (Table 41). The majority of out-migrants
from MM went to MR. In turn, MR migrants mostly went to FR and MM.
MM was also the favored destination for migrants from LR. And, again,
at least half of FR migrants merely transferred from one frontier region
to another, although a bigger share than before moved to MR.

Table 42 illustrates that MM and FR were highly preferred destinations
of the 1960-1970 streams, even when population sizes at origin and destinations are taken into account. Some shifts occurred, however, from the
pattern of the earlier lifetime streams. The MR-MM stream dropped in
relative intensity, while the LR-MM stream became more intense. The
relative intensities of the streams from MM to MR, LR, and FR increased
markedly. The intensity within FR decreased, while that to the other
destinations rose.

To summarize, the data suggest no clear relationship between the interregional patterns of migration and urbanization. While the metro region
was the preferred destination of most streams, the frontier regions were

favored over the more urbanized regions. The more urbanized regions were both major sources and recipients of migrants. At any rate, the less urbanized regions seemed to be the least attractive to both their residents and migrants from other regions. Undoubtedly, they had the relative disadvantage of having no extra resources or economic growth.

BROAD STREAMS AND COUNTERSTREAMS

From the interregional matrices in Tables 35 and 39 we can glean just the dominant streams and corresponding counterstreams for lifetime and recent period migrations. In this section, we attempt to assess the net effectiveness of the different streams. To what extent are population flows in one direction offset by flows in the opposite direction? Are flows from less urbanized regions more effective than those from more urbanized regions? Do migration interchanges increase with time; conversely, are more recent streams less effective than older streams?

We noted in the preceding section that the less urbanized and more urbanized regions were the principal origins, while the metropolitan and frontier regions were the main destinations of migration streams. The dominant streams and the ratios to their corresponding counterstreams for birth-1960 and 1960-1970 migrations are the following:

Stream	Birth-1960	1960-1970
MR - MM	9.92	2.25
MR - FR	28.46	5.47
LR - MM	15.07	3.39
LR - MR	1.47	1.93
LR - FR	11.45	5.01
FR - MM	2.33	1.31

With FR as the destination, streams from MR were more effective than those from LR, but with MM as the destination the opposite was true. A comparison of lifetime with recent migration shows that interregional migration reciprocity apparently increased with time and virtually all streams became measurably less effective. For instance, whereas about twenty-eight lifetime migrants from MR to FR were countered by only one reverse migrant, in 1960-1970 the ratio was only 5 to 1. Similarly, the dominant lifetime stream from LR to MM of 15 to 1 declined appreciably to only 3 to 1 for the recent stream. Only the comparatively weak stream between LR and MR (ratio of 1.5) stayed roughly the same.

Another measure of stream effectiveness or, conversely, interregional reciprocity is the index of effectiveness. It looks at net gain as a percentage of gross interchange, as shown below for the same streams:[6]

Stream	Birth-1960	1960-1970
MR - MM	81.7	38.5
MR - FR	93.2	69.1
LR - MM	87.6	54.4
LR - MR	19.1	31.8
LR - FR	83.9	66.7
FR - MM	39.9	13.5
Total	80.0	49.9

The interstream effectiveness differentials seem narrower, but the same streams figure prominently. Likewise, it is evident that the recent period has seen greater interchange and mutuality between the major regions.[7] Overall, the index of migration effectiveness fell from 80 for lifetime to 50 for recent period migration.

RURAL-URBAN STREAMS

While some relationships between migration and urbanization in a broad interregional context emerged from the above analysis, the patterns were not very clear. One disadvantage in the migration framework used is that some migrants to the more urbanized regions, for example, may in fact go to the rural areas of these regions, or some of those who go to the less urbanized regions may really settle in their urban areas; likewise, from the standpoint of the regions of origin. It is possible to cull data on rural/urban/metropolitan streams from the 1973 NDS. In this section, we inspect these kinds of streams and raise similar questions to those raised previously.

Lifetime and recent period migrations according to the three chief locales of origin and destination are given in Table 43. In this context,

TABLE 43
Birth-1965 and 1965-1973 Migrations
by Origin and Destination

| | Locale of Residence, 1965 and 1973 | | | |
	Rural	Urban	Metro	Total
Locale of Birth	Birth-1965			
Rural	1,581,755	1,436,877	602,794	3,621,426
Urban	461,997	255,785	149,457	867,239
Metro	83,127	41,494	173,741	298,362
Total	2,126,879	1,734,156	925,992	4,787,027
Locale of Residence	1965-1973			
1965				
Rural	594,290	757,891	432,824	1,785,005
Urban	312,714	180,085	126,543	619,342
Metro	125,970	85,294	374,206	585,470
Total	1,032,974	1,023,270	933,573	2,989,817

Note: Metropolitan is the formally accepted definition, but the rural and urban definitions are different from the 1963 Census definitions used in the earlier chapters. The 1973 NDS rural refers to all *barrios,* while urban refers to all *poblaciones* and cities outside Metro Manila.

The numbers refer to migrants 15 years old and over.

SOURCE: 1973 NDS.

it appears that a smaller majority of both lifetime and period migrants (fifteen years old and over) changed their general locales of residence, 58.0 and 61.6 percent, respectively, compared to the interregional streams. In other words, a good number of migrants moved within the same general locale.

The relative sizes (in percent) of the nine lifetime and period streams can be calculated from Table 43 as follows:

Stream	Birth-1965	1965-1973
Rural-Rural	33.0	19.9
Rural-Urban	30.0	25.3
Rural-Metro	12.6	14.5
Urban-Rural	9.6	10.4
Urban-Urban	5.3	6.0
Urban-Metro	3.1	4.2
Metro-Rural	1.7	4.2
Metro-Urban	0.9	2.8
Metro-Metro	3.6	12.5
Total	100.0	100.0

Thus, of the older streams the most sizable were rural-rural, rural-urban, and rural-metro, in that order, altogether accounting for over three-fourths of the total volume of migration. In the more recent period, the rural-urban stream became more important than the rural-rural flow, but both streams diminished in overall dominance as all the other streams gained some significance. There was less mobility from rural areas, greater movement between urban areas, and greater movement from the urban and metro locales to the rural scene.

Examining the dominant streams vis-à-vis their counterstreams, the following ratios obtain:

	Stream/Counterstream	
Stream	Birth-1965	1965-1973
Rural-Urban	3.11	2.42
Rural-Metro	7.25	3.44
Urban-Metro	3.60	1.48

There was a clear diminution in stream intensity over time. For instance, rural-metro, which was the strongest of the lifetime streams, weakened from 7.2 migrants per 1.0 reverse migrant for birth-1965 to 3.4 for 1965-1973.

The heightened interchange between locales is further evinced by declining indices of effectiveness (in percent) for the same streams:

Stream	Birth-1965	1965-1973
Rural-Urban	51.3	41.6
Rural-Metro	75.8	54.9
Urban-Metro	56.5	19.5
Total	57.7	43.1

The drop in the effectiveness of the streams is striking, particularly that for urban-metro. It is instructive to note, moreover, that the net locale transfers, which these three streams generated, involved only about 1,602,000 lifetime migrants, just about one-third of all lifetime migrants. The proportion of recent migration that brought about net locale redistribution declined even further to just over one-fourth, or 793,000 migrants. In terms of net consequence for overall urbanization, net rural-urban and rural-metro streams together accounted for only 31 and 25 percent of all lifetime and recent migration streams, respectively.

SUMMARY AND CONCLUSION

The patterns of internal migration indicate that spatial mobility has largely entailed not only long-distance movements between regions but also transfers from one socioeconomic type of milieu to another. Metro Manila has been the prime destination of streams from both the more urbanized and less urbanized regions. The frontier regions likewise gained a great deal from these two sources and experienced much intrafrontier transfer. The more urbanized regions also attracted migrants, especially from the less urbanized regions. The less urbanized regions appeared to be the least attractive to both their own natives or residents and migrants from other regions. While most lifetime streams were highly effective, interregional migration reciprocity increased with time as recent counterstreams became significantly stronger.

Lifetime rural-rural flows were relatively more voluminous than rural-urban flows, but this was reversed for recent migration. Also, more recently, there was greater mutuality between urban areas, within the metro area, as well as between urban and metro areas, on the one hand, and the rural environs, on the other. Therefore, the diminished net effectiveness of rural-urban and rural-metro streams has meant a smaller net effect of migration on rural-urban population transfers or on the urbanization process, a finding which agrees with the earlier conclusion of slower urbanization tempo more recently than in the earlier periods.

ANNEX

TABLE C

Regional Lifetime Migration, 1960 and 1970
(in thousands)

Region	Birth-1960			Birth-1970		
	In	Out	Net	In	Out	Net
Manila City	504	315	+189	522	454	+68
More Urbanized	1,143	2,026	−883	2,020	2,762	−742
Central Luzon	151	567	−416	296	758	−462
Southern Luzon	844	174	+670	1,478	258	+1,220
Western Visayas	70	500	−430	106	690	−584
Central Visayas	79	785	−706	140	1,055	−915
Less Urbanized	170	742	−572	292	1,246	−954
Ilocos	51	229	−178	78	365	−287
Bicol	82	208	−126	135	375	−240
Eastern Visayas	37	304	−267	79	506	−427
Frontier	1,634	369	+1,265	2,089	463	+1,626
Cagayan	163	62	+101	214	99	+115
Western Mindanao	395	37	+358	354	79	+275
Northern Mindanao	351	236	+115	531	205	+326
Southern Mindanao	724	34	+690	990	80	+910
Philippines	3,452	3,452	0	4,924	4,924	0

SOURCE: NCSO, 1960 and 1970 censuses.

TABLE D

Regional Period Migration, 1960-1970

Region	In-Migration	Out-Migration	Net Migration
Manila City	238,796	514,529	−275,733
More Urbanized	1,249,561	1,123,883	+125,678
Central Luzon	207,627	293,297	−85,670
Southern Luzon	859,595	188,690	+670,905
Western Visayas	75,431	278,832	−203,401
Central Visayas	106,908	363,064	−256,156
Less Urbanized	217,478	552,305	−334,827
Ilocos	55,660	136,370	−80,710
Bicol	98,730	179,925	−81,195
Eastern Visayas	63,088	236,010	−172,922
Frontier	843,584	358,702	+484,882
Cagayan	81,922	59,283	+22,639
Western Mindanao	123,379	73,236	+50,143
Northern Mindanao	274,066	126,213	+147,853
Southern Mindanao	364,217	99,970	+264,247
Philippines	2,549,419	2,549,419	

Note: Children below 10 years of age (from place of birth data) are included.
SOURCE: NCSO, 1970 Census.

TABLE E

Philippines: Population by Broad Regions of Birth and Residence in 1960

Region of Birth	Region of Residence, 1960				Total
	Metro Manila	More Urbanized	Less Urbanized	Frontier	
Metro Manila	1,547,269	84,722	21,424	22,933	1,676,348
More Urbanized	840,371	11,677,756	113,900	1,118,321	13,750,348
Less Urbanized	322,900	167,738	5,709,962	237,241	6,437,841
Frontier	53,437	39,297	20,720	5,028,660	5,142,114
Total	2,763,977	11,969,513	5,866,006	6,407,155	22,006,651

SOURCE: NCSO, 1960 Census.

TABLE F

Philippines: Population 10 Years Old and Over by Broad Regions of Residence in 1960 and 1970

Region of Residence 1960	Region of Residence, 1970				
	Metro Manila	More Urbanized	Less Urbanized	Frontier	Total
Metro Manila	2,371,277	156,598	68,734	37,208	2,633,817
More Urbanized	352,593	10,617,248	64,471	386,601	11,420,913
Less Urbanized	232,910	124,588	4,547,017	107,742	5,012,257
Frontier	48,842	70,711	21,501	5,867,632	6,008,686
Total	3,005,622	10,969,145	4,701,723	6,399,183	25,075,673

SOURCE: NCSO, 1970 Census.

NOTES

1. This indicates the proportion of the population of all ages enumerated in a province or region other than its province or region of birth. For the period 1960-1970, 8.0 percent of the population in 1970 were found in a region different from their 1960 region of residence.

2. The 1960 data are based on a 0.5 percent, and the 1970 data on a 5.0 percent, systematic sample of all households.

3. The 1970 Census migration data are given by rural-urban destinations but not by rural-urban origins.

4. Because of data constraints, the metro region here comprises Manila City and Rizal province, which is a close approximation of the formally accepted metro definition used elsewhere.

5. Index of preference, $\text{IPR} = \dfrac{M_{ij}}{M\left(\dfrac{p_i}{P} \cdot \dfrac{p_j}{P}\right)} \cdot k$

See U.N. Manual VI, pp. 48-49.

6. Symbolically, index of effectiveness,

$$I_e = \frac{M_{ij} - M_{ji}}{M_{ij} + M_{ji}} \cdot k$$

The U.N. Manual VI (1970:49) uses the absolute value for the numerator, but since we are interested here in the dominant streams we use net gain for the numerator.

7. A similar observation of reduced stream effectiveness with time was pointed out by Smith (1975a) with respect to the twelve regions or the three large regions of Luzon, Visayas, and Mindanao.

CHARACTERISTICS OF MIGRATION STREAMS

6

More significant perhaps than the sheer numbers of people who move are the types of people who constitute the different migration streams. In this chapter, we attempt to examine the characteristics of the principal migration streams that were identified in the preceding chapter. We address ourselves to the following quesitons: (1) how different are the rural-urban streams from the other major streams; (2) are migrants better off or worse off than those left behind; and, (3) how do migrants fare in the place of destination?

Many believe that it is not only the volume but also the inferior quality of rural-urban migrants that has caused problems for urban areas as well as for the nation as a whole.[1] More recent researches into the causes and consequences of rural-urban migration (mostly carried out by looking into the characteristics of migrants) have, however, come up with findings that are quite surprisingly the contrary. For example, Carvajal and Geithman (1974) interpreted migration in Costa Rica as a rational economic response to intersectoral differences in opportunities, as shown by empirical evidence that both recent and settled migrants earn significantly higher incomes and are also better off in other respects than nonmigrants. In like manner, Feitosa (1975), utilizing Philippine data from the 1968 National Demographic Survey, found that migrants are better educated and have higher average occupational achievements than nonmigrants at origin. In comparison with those at destination, migrants have lower educational and occupational levels, but these shortcomings tend to disappear with length of exposure to the urban environment. Focusing on fertility differentials, Hendershot (1971) invoked the social-mobility theory to explain why rural-to-Manila migrants are positively selected, why they participate in urban practices at least to the same extent as natives, and why migrants have lower fertility than natives.

The purpose of this chapter is to demonstrate further that rural-urban migration is not necessarily a negative aspect of development. This is because migrants are positively selected and tend to be upwardly mobile in urban areas. The degree of positive selectivity and upward mobility tends to be directly related to the level of urbanization and development of the destination area. For instance, migrants who go to the metro area are better off than those who go to other types of regions because they are more positively selected to start with, and therefore have better chances of success at the destination.

In order to appreciate the differentials between the different types of migrants and those who do not migrate, we make use of data from the 1970 Census and the 1973 National Demographic Survey. We focus on basic demographic characteristics of sex and age as well as on key socioeconomic traits as reflected in educational attainment and income levels. Survey data on migration characteristics refer to the time around 1973, not at the time of migration. In this way, they are more indicative of the consequences than of the causes or selectivity of migration. This is especially true of lifetime migration; but period migration, to the extent that the interval covered is short, can also shed light on selectivity at the place of origin. We must also point out that survey data can provide information on migrants found at destination at the time of survey, not on migrants who may have returned for one reason or other. In other words, we may be dealing with a select group of migrants who have succeeded and therefore stayed at their destination. This would exert a bias in comparing migrants with nonmigrants.

We start by making broad comparisons between recent migrants, old migrants, and nonmigrants or the general population as points of reference. Then we assess the differentials of the major interregional and rural-urban streams. Likewise, we compare the migrants in the various streams to nonmigrants at origin and destination.

OVERVIEW OF DIFFERENTIALS

Selectivity according to age can be safely considered a universal law of migration. Philippine migration is no exception to the rule, as attested by

Table 44. It shows that migrants are positively selected at young adult ages—around twenty to forty in the case of males and fifteen to thirty-five in the case of females. At all other ages the selection is negative. Age selectivity is more intense for females than for males as denoted by a higher coefficient of dissimilarity for the former.

With respect to sex, there is no universality; rather, there are regional variations across the world and even intercountry differences within re-

TABLE 44

Age Distribution of 1965-1970 Migrants and of Total Population
in 1970 and Indices of Differentials (in percent)

Age	Males			Females		
	Migrants	Total Population	Index[1]	Migrants	Total Population	Index
0-4	11.8	17.3	−32	10.0	16.6	−40
5-9	12.0	15.5	−23	9.3	14.7	−36
10-14	9.1	14.0	−35	9.2	13.4	−44
15-19	10.7	10.9	−1	18.1	11.4	+59
20-24	14.9	8.4	+78	18.2	8.8	+107
25-29	13.3	6.5	+104	11.8	6.9	+70
30-34	9.2	5.5	+68	7.1	5.8	+22
35-39	6.2	5.2	+19	4.6	5.2	−19
40-44	3.9	4.0	−5	3.0	4.1	−27
45-49	2.7	3.4	−20	2.2	3.6	−39
50-54	1.9	2.8	−33	1.7	2.8	−39
55-59	1.5	2.8	−46	1.4	2.2	−37
60+	2.8	4.4	−38	2.8	4.6	−38
Total	100.0	100.0	18.1[2]	100.0	100.0	22.3

1. Difference between the two distributions as percent of the proportion of population in that age group for the total population.

2. Sum of the positive differences between the two distributions (coefficient of dissimilarity).

SOURCE: NCSO, 1970 Census.

gions. For example, in African countries males are generally more migratory than females. In Latin America and in many Asian countries, the reverse is true. In the Philippines, women have a higher propensity to migrate than men, as illustrated in Table 45 by the low sex ratios at migratory ages for all three kinds of migrants in comparison with the total population. The differential is most pronounced in the age group fifteen to nineteen where the number of recent male migrants is just over half of female migrants. Table 45 also suggests that, with time, women increase their propensity

TABLE 45

Sex Ratio of Migrants and Total Population,
by Age (males per 1,000 females)

| Age | Migrants | | | Total 1970 |
	1965-1970	1960-1970	Lifetime	Population
0-4	1,069	1,069	1,069	1,028
5-9	1,090	1,076	1,076	1,041
10-14	893	931	977	1,027
15-19	536	593	689	945
20-24	741	739	801	939
25-29	1,022	977	988	935
30-34	1,180	1,145	1,090	946
35-39	1,204	1,207	1,124	981
40-44	1,187	1,121	1,049	972
45-49	1,111	1,088	994	953
50-54	982	1,020	989	977
55-59	982	955	994	995
60-64	875	952	1,102	1,029
65-69	999	956	1,126	973
70-79	850	952	1,151	1,062
75+	779	804	1,042	867
All	903	921	964	990

SOURCE: NCSO, 1970 Census.

TABLE 46

Mean Years of Schooling: Recent Migrants,
Settled Migrants, and Nonmigrants, 1973

Sex/Age	Recent	Settled	Nonmigrants
Both Sexes			
15+	7.8	6.7	6.2
15-34	8.5	7.9	7.4
Males			
15+	7.9	6.9	6.3
15-34	8.5	8.0	7.3
Females			
15+	7.7	6.5	6.1
15-34	8.4	7.9	7.5

SOURCE: 1973 NDS.

to migrate and become more dominant. Female dominance in Philippine migration seems to be promoted by the fact that Filipino women are comparatively highly educated (practically as much as Filipino men, as will be seen below) and can therefore easily find clerical jobs or service occupations in cities. Moreover, females are less useful on the farms than are males.

In terms of educational attainment, survey data show the highest level for recent (1965-1973) migrants, followed by settled (birth-1965) migrant and nonmigrants, in that order[2] (Table 46). The differentials persist for males or females separately and for the prime adult ages of fifteen to thirty-four years.

The pattern is different insofar as income is concerned. Although the status of a migrant is still significantly advantageous over that of a nonmigrant, settled migrants appear to have an income edge over recent migrants, as shown by Table 47. This may be logical to the extent that settled migrants, by definition, have had the time to adjust to the income

TABLE 47

Mean Cash Income: Recent Migrants, Settled Migrants,
and Nonmigrants, 1972 (in pesos)

Sex/Age	Recent	Settled	Nonmigrants
Both Sexes			
15+	1,410.0	1,536.2	1,112.0
15-34	1,212.5	1,263.6	963.0
Males			
15+	2,013.2	2,110.3	1,395.8
15-34	1,691.3	1,673.5	1,118.8
Females			
15+	915.8	980.1	818.7
15-34	856.7	876.3	792.6

SOURCE: 1973 NDS.

opportunities of the new place. The income differentials between the three statuses remain even when the effects of sex or age are controlled (except for the apparent reversal in advantage from settled to recent male migrants aged fifteen to thirty-four). Table 47 also shows that, unlike educational attainment, average incomes are lower at younger ages.[3]

INTERREGIONAL STREAM DIFFERENTIALS

The broad interregional migration matrix in the previous chapter provided a total of sixteen different streams. Here we concentrate on the six streams that were identified as dominant. The number of migrants in these streams account for about 47 and 60 percent, respectively, of all lifetime and recent interregional migrants.

TABLE 48

Age Distribution by Sex for Dominant Interregional Streams, 1965-1973 (in percent)

Stream	15-24	25-34	35-49	50+	Total (100 pct.)
			Both Sexes		
MR-MM	58.9	20.0	14.8	6.4	303,589
MR-FR	44.4	21.0	27.1	7.5	196,092
LR-MM	66.7	16.1	7.7	9.4	206,194
LR-MR	55.7	17.9	15.3	11.1	78,440
LR-FR	34.7	23.4	21.5	20.4	56,866
FR-MM	57.5	25.7	9.5	7.3	49,584
			Males		
MR-MM	58.6	18.1	17.4	6.0	118,429
MR-FR	40.4	24.9	24.9	9.9	98,979
LR-MM	59.2	25.4	7.0	8.4	73,254
LR-MR	42.8	17.9	26.9	12.5	30,436
LR-FR	31.9	18.1	32.1	17.9	27,136
FR-MM	45.2	35.8	11.0	8.0	18,517
			Females		
MR-MM	59.0	21.2	13.1	6.6	185,160
MR-FR	48.4	17.0	29.5	5.1	97,113
LR-MM	70.9	11.0	8.1	10.0	132,940
LR-MR	63.9	18.0	8.0	10.2	48,004
LR-FR	37.2	28.2	11.9	22.7	29,730
FR-MM	64.8	19.7	8.6	6.9	31,067

Note: MM - Metro Manila, MR = more urbanized regions, LR = less urbanized regions, and FR = frontier regions. Total absolute numbers are the total weighted cases for the streams, the average weight being 790.4621.
SOURCE: 1973 NDS.

TABLE 49

Age Distribution by Sex for Dominant Interregional Streams,
Birth-1965 (in percent)

Stream	15-24	25-34	35-49	50+	Total (100 pct.)
			Both Sexes		
MR-MM	18.3	23.7	31.8	26.1	486,527
MR-FR	16.8	19.9	36.4	27.0	1,061,933
LR-MM	19.6	30.1	30.9	19.4	232,852
LR-MR	22.6	17.6	41.1	18.7	198,903
LR-FR	11.0	21.0	40.2	27.7	226,160
FR-MM	18.0	31.0	34.4	16.7	32,872
			Males		
MR-MM	17.3	22.8	32.3	27.7	233,127
MR-FR	17.0	18.8	35.3	28.9	558,534
LR-MM	22.3	23.2	29.4	25.2	101,401
LR-MR	17.8	22.2	35.6	24.5	97,116
LR-FR	12.3	16.6	31.2	40.0	114,828
FR-MM	25.4	33.9	33.3	7.4	16,243
			Females		
MR-MM	19.3	24.5	31.5	24.7	253,400
MR-FR	16.6	21.1	37.5	24.8	503,399
LR-MM	17.6	35.4	32.0	15.0	131,451
LR-MR	27.1	13.3	46.4	13.2	101,787
LR-FR	9.7	25.5	49.6	15.1	111,332
FR-MM	10.8	28.1	35.4	25.7	16,629

Note: MM = Metro Manila, MR = more urbanized regions, LR = less urbanized regions, and FR = frontier regions. Total absolute numbers are the total weighted cases for the streams, the average weight being 790.4621.

SOURCE: 1973 NDS.

TABLE 50

Age Distribution by Sex for Nonmigrants by Type of Region, 1973 (in percent)

Region Type	15-24	25-34	35-49	50+	Total (100 pct.)
Both Sexes					
Metro Manila	48.9	20.1	17.4	13.6	928,091
More Urbanized	38.5	19.0	23.0	19.4	7,591,664
Less Urbanized	33.4	22.6	24.1	19.9	2,893,229
Frontier	45.9	19.3	22.7	12.0	2,937,771
Males					
Metro Manila	51.5	20.0	16.6	11.9	458,276
More Urbanized	40.3	18.4	21.6	19.7	3,732,199
Less Urbanized	36.0	21.3	22.4	20.3	1,464,747
Frontier	45.3	18.9	23.6	12.1	1,459,925
Females					
Metro Manila	46.4	20.1	18.1	15.4	469,815
More Urbanized	36.8	19.7	24.3	19.1	3,859,465
Less Urbanized	30.8	24.0	25.8	19.4	1,428,482
Frontier	46.5	19.8	21.8	11.9	1,477,846

Note: Total absolute numbers are the total weighted cases, the average weight being 790.4621.

SOURCE: 1973 NDS.

Tables 48-50 present the age distributions for recent and lifetime inter-regional streams as well as nonmigrants by locale of residence. Among the recent streams, those destined to the metro area (wherever the origin) are visibly dominated by young adults aged fifteen to twenty-four. Recent migrants are younger compared to nonmigrants both in the metro area and in the regions of origin. Settled migrants are generally older (as would be expected), but, between lifetime streams, those going to the metropolitan and more urbanized regions are younger than frontierward movers.

TABLE 51

Sex Ratios for Recent Migrants, Lifetime Migrants,
and Nonmigrants, by Age (males per 1,000 females)

Stream	15-24	25-34	35-49	50+	Total
			1965-1973 Migrants		
MR-MM	635	546	845	575	640
MR-FR	851	1,488	859	1,976	1,019
LR-MM	460	1,279	477	458	551
LR-MR	424	631	2,136	779	634
LR-FR	782	585	2,469	721	913
FR-MM	416	1,085	760	691	596
			Birth-1965 Migrants		
MR-MM	825	855	943	1,029	920
MR-FR	1,132	989	1,044	1,296	1,110
LR-MM	974	505	710	1,292	771
LR-MR	626	1,595	731	1,766	954
LR-FR	1,307	668	648	2,724	1,031
FR-MM	2,299	1,177	920	281	977
Region Type			Nonmigrants		
Metro Manila	1,083	971	894	752	975
More Urbanized	1,057	901	859	998	967
Less Urbanized	1,199	912	887	1,073	1,025
Frontier	962	944	1,072	1,008	988

SOURCE: 1973 NDS.

The corresponding sex ratios are given in Table 51. Recent streams to
the metro area from less urbanized and frontier regions are markedly
female-dominated (low sex ratios) for reasons already cited above. Those
to the more urbanized regions are less heavily weighted by females, and
those to frontier regions are more male-dominated. The same pattern can
be observed from the older lifetime streams, although the sex ratios are

TABLE 52

Mean Years of Schooling: Interregional Streams, 1965-1973
and Birth-1965

Sex/Age	MR-MM	MR-FR	LR-MM	LR-MR	LR-FR	FR-MM
			1965-1973			
Both Sexes						
15+	9.0	6.2	8.4	6.7	5.8	9.9
15-34	9.4	7.0	8.8	7.5	7.6	9.8
Males						
15+	9.8	6.7	9.5	6.1	5.1	10.1
15-34	10.1	7.4	9.8	7.3	7.3	9.6
Females						
15+	8.5	5.7	7.7	7.1	6.4	9.8
15-34	9.0	6.7	8.2	7.6	7.8	9.8
			Birth-1965			
Both Sexes						
15+	9.1	5.1	8.5	6.7	5.7	9.6
15-34	10.4	6.2	9.1	7.8	7.2	10.1
Males						
15+	9.9	5.2	9.5	6.8	5.5	10.1
15-34	11.0	6.2	10.2	8.2	6.7	9.3
Females						
15+	8.4	4.9	7.8	6.6	5.9	9.2
15-34	9.9	6.2	8.3	7.5	7.6	11.2

SOURCE: 1973 NDS.

generally higher than those for recent migration. This confirms an earlier observation from census data (Table 45) concerning the rise of female migration over time.

With regard to educational attainment, Table 52 shows that selectivity depends more on where migrants go to than where they come from. Thus,

TABLE 53

Mean Years of Schooling: Nonmigrants by Type of Region, 1973

Sex/Age	Metro	More Urbanized	Less Urbanized	Frontier
Both Sexes				
15+	9.6	6.2	5.6	5.7
15-34	10.5	7.5	6.8	6.8
Males				
15+	9.9	6.3	5.7	5.8
15-34	10.4	7.4	6.7	6.8
Females				
15+	9.4	6.1	5.6	5.7
15-34	10.6	7.6	7.0	6.8

SOURCE: 1973 NDS.

all migrants to Metro Manila are relatively highly educated whether they originate in the more urbanized, less urbanized, or frontier regions. This remains true even when region of origin is controlled, that is, migrants from the less urbanized regions to different types of destinations are compared. Controlling for age does not materially alter the relative differentials but merely shows that the education of younger migrants is higher. The same pattern of differentials is evident for the older streams (Table 52, lower half).

A comparison with the mean years of schooling of nonmigrants (Table 53) suggests that native metropolitanites are slightly better educated than in-migrants from whatever region. The other in-migrants, however, are at least as educated as, if not more than, the nonmigrants at destination (with the seeming exception of lifetime migrants in frontier regions).

In terms of cash income, frontier-metro migrants appear to have the highest mean incomes, even higher than of those who originate in the more urbanized regions. This is true for both recent and lifetime migrants

TABLE 54

Mean Cash Income: Interregional Streams,
1965-1973 and Birth-1965 (in pesos)

Sex/Age	MR-MM	MR-FR	LR-MM	LR-MR	LR-FR	FR-MM
			1965-1973			
Both Sexes						
15+	1,476.5	888.4	1,091.5	909.3	1,161.6	1,606.6
15-34	1,145.2	770.6	995.2	787.8	1,136.3	1,135.1
Males						
15+	2,200.5	1,164.4	1,796.3	1,495.2	1,415.5	2,722.7
15-34	1,678.5	976.4	1,498.7	1,324.4	1,017.7	1,927.3
Females						
15+	1,033.9	605.1	716.9	516.6	904.8	860.7
15-34	837.8	563.6	725.8	520.4	1,227.1	630.6
			Birth-1965			
Both Sexes						
15+	2,489.3	1,098.5	2,314.1	1,538.0	1,388.8	2,945.6
15-34	2,029.5	906.7	2,030.4	1,242.8	1,257.3	2,646.1
Males						
15+	3,662.6	1,458.2	3,490.5	2,297.4	1,817.0	4,224.4
15-34	2,851.7	1,155.2	2,832.5	1,794.5	1,458.6	3,322.8
Females						
15+	1,378.5	678.2	1,412.1	839.0	931.9	1,457.5
15-34	1,284.6	603.5	1,509.9	679.8	1,067.4	1,220.5

SOURCE: 1973 NDS.

(Table 54). An inspection of the income situation of nonmigrants (Table 55) reveals that the metro nonmigrants have higher incomes than recent in-migrants but lower than settled migrants. More urbanized nonmigrants

TABLE 55

Mean Cash Income: Nonmigrants by Type of Region,
1973 (in pesos)

Sex/Age	Metro Manila	More Urbanized	Less Urbanized	Frontier
Both Sexes				
15+	1,852.2	1,115.2	942.2	1,059.4
15-34	1,447.2	987.9	859.9	838.0
Males				
15+	2,302.0	1,410.0	1,134.5	1,371.7
15-34	1,593.9	1,173.2	969.9	978.1
Females				
15+	1,396.2	824.3	731.4	716.0
15-34	1,284.5	792.2	727.6	686.4

SOURCE: 1973 NDS.

are better off than out-migrants to other than metro regions but inferior
to settled in-migrants. Finally, out-migrants from less urbanized regions
to whatever destination are generally more successful than those who are
not mobile.

INTERSECTORAL STREAM DIFFERENTIALS

In addition to the three dominant intersectoral streams that were
singled out in the previous chapter, we also examine here rural-rural flow,
which was the largest of all lifetime streams and the second largest of all
period migrations. These four streams constitute approximately 79 and
64 percent, respectively, of all lifetime and recent intersectoral (rural-
urban) migrants.

Table 56 shows once again that educational level is a function of both
origin and destination of migrants. Accordingly, urban-metro migrants

TABLE 56

Mean Years of Schooling: Intersectoral Streams,
1965-1973 and Birth-1965

Sex/Age	R-R	R-U	R-M	U-M
		1965-1973		
Both Sexes				
15+	5.4	7.9	8.8	9.9
15-34	6.3	8.6	9.2	10.2
Males				
15+	5.2	7.8	10.0	10.5
15-34	6.0	8.4	10.0	10.4
Females				
15+	5.6	8.0	8.3	9.5
15-34	6.7	8.8	8.7	10.0
		Birth-1965		
Both Sexes				
15+	4.9	7.2	8.7	9.5
15-34	6.1	8.3	10.0	10.3
Males				
15+	5.0	7.6	9.3	10.2
15-34	6.1	8.3	10.6	10.7
Females				
15+	4.7	6.9	8.0	8.8
15-34	6.1	8.4	9.4	9.9

Note: R = rural, U = urban, and M = metropolitan.
SOURCE: 1973 NDS.

TABLE 57

Mean Years of Schooling: Nonmigrants by Locale, 1973

Sex/Age	Rural	Urban	Metro
Both Sexes			
15+	5.4	7.8	9.7
15-34	6.6	8.8	10.5
Males			
15+	5.5	7.9	9.9
15-34	6.6	8.7	10.4
Females			
15+	5.3	7.7	9.5
15-34	6.7	8.9	10.6

SOURCE: 1973 NDS.

have the highest mean years of schooling, followed by rural-metro, rural-urban, and rural-rural migrants, in that order. This pattern is true for both recent and settled migrants, even when age or sex is controlled. However, average educational level is generally lower for the older migrants (as also observed earlier), and recent female migrants to other than the metro destination are somewhat better educated than their male counterparts.

A comparison with nonmigrants in Table 57 shows that recent rural-rural migrants are as schooled as rural nonmigrants, but migrants to urban and metro areas are clearly better educated. Rural-urban migrants have about the same level of schooling as urban natives. Rural-metro migrants are less schooled than metro natives, but the male migrants are just as schooled as the male metro nonmigrants. Urban-metro migrants are better educated than metro natives and significantly more so than those who stay behind. The superiority of migrants to a locale different from origin to those left behind is also true of lifetime movers.

Data on cash income (Tables 58 and 59) show a pattern of differentials between streams similar to that for education, although the educational

TABLE 58

Mean Cash Income: Intersectoral Streams, 1965-1973
and Birth-1965 (in pesos)

Sex/Age	R-R	R-U	R-M	U-M
		1965-1973		
Both Sexes				
15+	856.7	1,158.6	1,134.8	1,567.1
15-34	858.7	1,133.8	1,106.2	1,785.2
Males				
15+	1,163.3	1,890.8	2.046.2	3,410.3
15-34	1,080.4	1,533.8	1,604.2	2,649.7
Females				
15+	599.4	891.6	1,004.5	1,333.8
15-34	608.4	903.4	807.3	1,175.8
		Birth-1965		
Both Sexes				
15+	997.9	1,376.0	1,765.9	1,525.9
15-34	966.8	1,275.5	2,048.0	1,626.2
Males				
15+	1,470.9	2,388.0	3,873.6	3,249.9
15-34	1,217.2	1,796.2	2,817.9	2,186.8
Females				
15+	695.6	1,028.7	1,384.8	1,360.3
15-34	673.8	813.6	1,398.9	1,129.5

SOURCE: 1973 NDS.

advantage of recent migrants over settled migrants does not obtain for income. The edge of rural-urban, rural-metro, and urban-metro migrants over those who stay behind is manifest for both new and old migrants.

TABLE 59

Mean Cash Income: Nonmigrants by Locale,
1973 (in pesos)

Sex/Age	Rural	Urban	Metro
Both Sexes			
15+	905.2	1,199.3	1,448.1
15-34	858.0	1,123.9	1,447.2
Males			
15+	1,230.1	1,708.4	2,304.5
15-34	1,013.8	1,291.4	1,593.9
Females			
15+	698.5	1,040.0	1,413.4
15-34	663.8	953.8	1,284.5

SOURCE: 1973 NDS.

Recent rural-rural migrants seem to be worse off, but the earlier ones are better off, than rural nonmigrants. Furthermore, the data on the older streams reveal that it is only a matter of time before migrants can approximate, or even surpass, the incomes of native urbanites or metropolitanites.

SUMMARY AND CONCLUSION

This chapter has shown that rural-urban migration was more a positive than a negative aspect of development. The reasons are that migrants were positively selected and that selection tended to be more intense the more urbanized and developed was the area of destination. As a consequence, migrants had a fair chance for success at the place of settlement. The data showed that, on the whole, the status of a migrant was better than that of a nonmigrant. Recent migrants were better schooled but obtained lower incomes than settled migrants. Migrants to Metro Manila were superior to migrants going elsewhere, and those destined to more urbanized areas were better off than those to less urbanized or rural areas. In-migrants were, on the average, as well off as native urbanites or metropolitanites. Some recent in-migrants appeared worse off than natives but, with time allowed for settling down, they could be on the same level as, or even superior to, the natives. In all cases, migrants from less urbanized or rural areas were significantly superior to those who stayed behind, a clear indication that rural-urban migration was a positive move at least for the migrants themselves. It also indicates that, on balance, backward communities have been losing their better qualified members, their "agents of change," instead of being relieved of excess labor. For example, on the basis of the 1973 NDS data, rural areas in the Philippines during 1965-1973 appear to have lost educational skills in terms of roughly 7.3 million "person-years of schooling" because the volume of rural-urban migrants was much larger than that of urban-rural migrants and because the average educational attainment of rural-urban migrants was higher. This may partly explain why the less urbanized regions or rural areas have remained underdeveloped and continue to suffer out-migration.

NOTES

1. See, e.g., Lerner (1967) and Nelson (1969).
2. Data on recent migrants are based on about 3,700 unweighted cases, settled migrants about 6,000 cases, and nonmigrants some 17,900 cases.
3. An inspection of noncash income suggests that settled migrants are the most favored, followed by nonmigrants and recent migrants, in that order. But we do not try to make much out of it since data on noncash income are of inferior quality.

THE FUTURE OF URBANIZATION

7

Our analysis of historical and recent urbanization provides some foundations for speculating about its future. This chapter will illustrate what might be the prospects of urbanization and urban growth under various assumptions. The focus will be the year 2000, which is about a generation away and which might be a reasonable long-term target for planning. After making estimates of prospective overall urbanization and urban growth, we proceed to project citification and city growth, and then metropolitan growth. Finally, we summarize the projections in order to show what the overall distribution of the population might be in 2000 A.D.

OVERALL URBANIZATION AND URBAN GROWTH

Three different tempos of urbanization (URGD, or urban-rural growth difference) were identified in Chapter 2, namely 1.7 percent in 1903-1939, 2.1 percent in 1939-1960, and 1.5 percent in 1960-1970. On the basis of these rates, we can depict different urbanization futures, following the URGD method of the United Nations (Manual VIII, 1974:36-44). The use of this method is facilitated by reference to a table of logistic curve,[1] given in Annex I of Manual VIII. Accordingly, three variants of urbanization levels (percent urban) may be foreseen as follows:[2]

Year	Slow	Moderate	Rapid
1970	32.9	32.9	32.9
1975	34.5	34.8	35.2
1980	36.1	36.6	37.5
1990	39.4	40.4	42.3
2000	42.8	44.3	47.2

Applying these urban proportions to the projected total population (medium series of the University of the Philippines Population Institute), we get corresponding urban and rural populations (in thousands):

Year	Slow		Moderate		Rapid	
	Urban	Rural	Urban	Rural	Urban	Rural
1970	12,123	24,726	12,123	24,726	12,123	24,726
1975	14,561	27,645	14,688	27,518	14,857	27,349
1980	17,457	30,901	17,699	30,659	18,134	30,224
1990	24,730	38,036	25,357	37,409	26,550	36,216
2000	33,714	45,056	34,895	43,875	37,179	41,591

The implied annual rates of growth (in percent) would be the following:

Year	Slow		Moderate		Rapid	
	Urban	Rural	Urban	Rural	Urban	Rural
1970-1975	3.73	2.26	3.91	2.16	4.15	2.04
1975-1980	3.69	2.25	3.80	2.18	4.07	2.00
1980-1990	3.54	2.10	3.66	2.01	3.89	1.81
1990-2000	3.15	1.71	3.24	1.61	3.42	1.39

Which of the three urbanization trajectories is the most probable will depend largely on the future pace of overall population growth and socio-economic development, as we have seen in earlier chapters. Nevertheless, there are reasons to believe that urbanization is not likely to continue its slow tempo of the 1960-1970 period but will pick up and follow the rapid or, at least, the moderate trajectory. First, there is already some indication from the preliminary results of the 1975 Census that overall population growth is slowing down. Second, development policy seems to be increasingly oriented toward agricultural development, which could mean measurable releases of farm labor. Throughout this chapter we therefore assume that future urbanization will follow the relatively rapid projection.

Rapid urbanization would mean that the urban proportion would increase by some fourteen percentage points to 47 percent by 2000 A.D.[3] This figure would be far below the level of 55 percent for the world as a whole, as projected by Davis (1972:122) using the medium constant-rate or the American model. More significantly, it would be below the threshold 50 percent level after which the absolute size of rural population normally starts to decline. Yet, urban population would be threefold at 37 million, which is slightly more than the national population in 1970, and rural population would increase by over two-thirds.

An instructive question is: what would urban growth be like in the next quarter century if total population growth were to cease after 1975 but urbanization were to proceed according to the relatively rapid trajectory? In other words, what would be the impact on urban growth of pure rural-urban migration? The urban and rural populations (in thousands) would be as follows:

Year	Urban	Rural
1975	14,857	27,349
1980	15,827	26,379
1990	17,853	24,353
2000	19.921	22,285

Urban growth would be only about one-third of the total urban in 1975, and urban population in the year 2000 just over one-half of what it would be otherwise. Since the absolute urban increment would be under a quarter of what it would be, we might say that roughly three-fourths of expected urban growth is imputable to sheer population growth. At the same time, the cumulative decrement of the rural population would be some 18 percent of the total rural in 1975.

Alternatively, we could ask: what would be the consequence on urban and rural growth if total population were to grow at half the expected rate? Total population is projected (medium series of the University of the Philippines Population Institute) to increase 86.6 percent by the year 2000. Assuming the same prospective urbanization and a rate of population increase at 43.3 percent in twenty-five years, we would see the following:

Year	Urban	Rural
1975	14,857	27,349
2000	28,547	31,934

Urban population would hardly double, or it would be just over three-quarters of the expected size. In other words, the addition to urban population would be about 61 percent of that anticipated, so that roughly two-fifths of urban size loss may be "gained" by a halving of total population growth.

CITIFICATION AND CITY GROWTH

Citification, or the rise in the proportion of the population living in cities of 100,000 or more, may be projected in a similar fashion as over-all urbanization. The tempo of citification was also relatively brisk during 1939-1960 (exponential rate of 2.9 percent) and slowed down during the 1960s (exponential rate of 1.5 percent). Adopting these parameters along with the logistic method of the U.N. Manual VIII, we can derive prospect citification levels (percent in cities), to wit:

Year	Slow	Rapid
1970	16.7	16.7
1975	17.7	18.7
1980	18.8	21.1
1990	21.2	26.3
2000	23.9	32.3

Translating these proportions into absolute numbers (city residents in thousands), we obtain the following:

Year	Slow	Rapid
1970	6,140	6,140
1975	7,470	7,892
1980	9,091	10,204
1990	13,306	16,507
2000	18,826	25,443

The respective annual growth rates (in percent) would be:

Interval	Slow	Rapid
1970-1975	4.00	5.15
1975-1980	4.00	5.27
1980-1990	3.88	4.93
1990-2000	3.53	4.42

The rapid assumption is probably more realistic than the slow for the same reasons that were adduced earlier with respect to the acceleration of urbanization. If this is the case, the level of citification would practical double in thirty years. It may still be significantly lower than the level of

39 percent for the world as a whole (Davis, 1972:123), but the dramatic effect can be readily seen in the absolute growth of the city population. Total city population in the year 2000 would be over fourfold its size in 1970, or even threefold according to the slower growth.

Again, we might ask the hypothetical question: what would be the consequence on city growth assuming no population growth after 1975 but with urbanization and citification proceeding as expected? Estimated city and other-urban or town populations (in thousands) are:

Year	City	Town
1975	7,892	6,965
2000	13,632	6,289

Both city and town populations would be approximately 54 percent of their expected sizes. Inasmuch as absolute city growth is only a third of what it would be otherwise, two-thirds of the anticipated increment can be attributed to population growth. If population growth is half of the projected rate, city population would be two and a half times bigger instead of more than three times in twenty-five years. That is, incremental city population would be only two-thirds of that expected, implying that a "saving" may be generated in terms of one-third city growth foregone.

METROPOLITAN GROWTH

Population in Metro Manila can also be projected by the logistic technique (U.N. Manual VIII, 1974:46-48). The metropolitan share of total urban population rose from 30.0 percent in 1960 to 32.8 percent in 1970. Assuming this logistic progression will occur in the subsequent thirty years, the proportions of urban population in the metro area and the corresponding absolute numbers of metropolitanites may be as follows:

Year	Metro Share (pct. of total urban)	Number (thousands)
1970	32.8	3,953
1975	34.5	5,126
1980	36.1	6,546
1990	39.2	10,408
2000	42.5	15,801

The metro share would climb by nearly ten percentage points and metro population would virtually quadruple in thirty years. It would be fully 62 percent of the projected total city population at the end of the century.[4] Such prospective metro growth may be untenable, however, because of resource constraints which manifest themselves even at the prese time. At the crudest level, for instance, metro density would increase fro 6,471 persons per square kilometer in 1970 to an imponderable 25,869 by 2000 A.D., assuming a constant metro areal definition. Therefore, a radical cessation or redistribution of such growth may be crucially neede

Assuming zero population growth after 1975 and the metro share of urban population as projected, the number of metropolitanites would increase merely two-thirds to 8,466,000 instead of treble to 15,801,000. In other words, new metro residents would amount to less than a third of the projected number, implying that the preponderant balance can be accounted for by population growth. If population growth is half of that projected, additional metro population would be two-thirds of what is anticipated.

SUMMARY AND CONCLUSION

We can combine the projections to illustrate the future distribution of the national population into rural, town, city, and metropolitan sectors.[5] With national population growing according to the medium variant and urbanization proceeding according to the rapid trajectory, the sectoral distribution of population would be:

	Rural	Town	City	Metro	Total
	(in percent)				
1975	64.8	16.5	6.6	12.1	100.0
2000	52.8	14.9	12.2	20.1	100.0
	(in thousands)				
1975	27,349	6,965	2,766	5,126	42,206
2000	41,591	11,736	9,642	15,801	78,770

Assuming the same distributional pattern but with total population (a) not growing or (b) growing at half the projected rate, the following popul. tion sizes (in thousands) would result by the year 2000:

	Rural	Town	City	Metro	Total
(a)	22,285	6,289	5,166	8,466	42,206
(b)	31,934	9.012	7,403	12,132	60,481

The no-growth assumption allows for an appreciation of how much of sectoral population increase is attributable to urbanization and how much to overall population growth (in percent):

	Rural	Town	City	Metro
Urbanization	−35.6	−14.2	34.9	31.3
Population Growth	135.6	114.2	65.1	68.7

The one-half-growth assumption can show the relative amount of population reduction from the absolute increment that would ensue for each sector if total population grows as expected (in percent):

	Rural	Town	City	Metro
Percent Reduction	67.8	57.1	32.6	34.4

These, in other words, represent the "savings" in sectoral growth stemming from a reduced overall growth. While these estimates may be purely hypothetical, they clearly demonstrate how a slower growth of the total population can make urban growth in general substantially more manageable without hampering the urbanization process. In fact, as historical evidence in Chapter 2 has shown, the country's urbanization (development) can proceed even faster than we have assumed in such a situation.

NOTES

1. Symbolically, the curve is expressed as $100 \dfrac{U_t}{T_t} = \dfrac{100\,e^{dt}}{1 + e^{dt}}$, where U_t and T_t stand for the urban population and total population at time t, respectively; dt is the differential of time or change in t; and e is the base of Naperian logarithms.

2. The assumed exponential rates of URGD are 1.4 percent for slow, 1.6 percent for moderate, and 2.0 percent for rapid. The exponential rates, which are required for the projection method, are necessarily lower than their corresponding annual rates indicated above.

3. The level would be 52.2 percent if the country follows the historical path taken by a fairly rapidly urbanizing province, Cavite, which is adjacent to Metro Manila.

4. The metro population would be slightly bigger (by 5 percent) if, alternatively, the 1960-1970 growth rate is assumed.

5. Note that town, city, and metro populations add up to total urban.

CONCLUSION

8

This study examines Philippine urbanization in a framework that relates it to population growth, socioeconomic development, and rural-urban migration. It is hypothesized that urbanization tends to be affected negatively by population growth and positively by development. In addition, it is expected that when population growth is rapid, rural-urban migration tends to be a minor component of urban growth at the national level and in subnational areas experiencing slow urbanization. Because of the favorable characteristics of migrants, it seems incorrect to suppose that rural-urban migration is a negative aspect of the development process.

SUMMARY OF FINDINGS

In a historical perspective, Philippine urbanization cannot be characterized as rapid. In fact, it has slowed down in recent times as a consequence of the acceleration of population growth that occurred mostly in the rural sector. In comparison, Western countries experienced faster urbanization in the late nineteenth and early twentieth centuries, although the growth of their urban populations was slower. In the context of contemporary Southeast and East Asian countries, recent Philippine urbanization can also be described as relatively slow, be it in terms of the proportion in all urban places or only in cities of 100,000 or more inhabitants.

Against the background of slackening national urbanization, urban concentration became increasingly acute as Metro Manila's share of total and urban population in 1970 mounted to 11 and 33 percent, respectively, from 3 and 25 percent in 1903. Its size of 3.9 million inhabitants was more than five times the combined sizes of the cities of Cebu, Iloilo, and Bacolod in 1970. Overall urban population did expand tremendously (from 1 million to 12 million in seven decades), but so did rural population (from 6.6 to 24.6 million).

Reclassification of places accounted for a significant portion of urban growth in earlier periods, but, later, natural increase became the biggest component. The impact of rural-urban migration on overall urban growth was always minor compared to natural increase. It was strongest (22 percent of urban growth) during the period of fastest urbanization (1939-1960) and weakest (only 11 percent) during 1960-1970. It scraped barely 16 percent of rural growth in the earlier period and 8 percent during the later period. Therefore, from the standpoints of both the urban and rural sectors, overall net population transfers cannot be considered massive, although they may have been so in absolute terms.

As expected, migration was a significant contributor to the growth of Metro Manila and other big cities (about 50 percent). In the other regions, migration's impact on urban size can be described as relatively slight to moderate at most. It was relatively more palpable in the more urbanized and frontier regions than in the less urbanized ones, which suffered large urban population losses through out-migration. Hence, on balance, the rise in urban population and urban proportion did not entail a great deal of rural-urban mobility as fertility stayed high and mortality declined drastically in urban areas. This is in stark contrast to the historical experience of developed countries where rural-urban migration was practically synonymous with urbanization.

An examination of the Philippine economy in the 1950s and 1960s reveals that its transformation was sluggish in contrast to that of neighboring Asian economies which experienced buoyant urbanization. Within the Philippines itself (excepting Metro Manila), more urbanized regions were more advanced than other regions in terms of demographic development (lower fertility and mortality), labor force industrialization, and income levels. Not surprisingly, these regions also evinced rapid urbanization tempos of over four times those experienced by the less urbanized and frontier regions, or nearly twice the national average. As a consequence, the disparity between regions outside Metro Manila widened over time. By 1970, the more urbanized group was 30 percent urban, while the others stagnated at between 18 and 20 percent, which is a temporal gap of about thirty-one years in terms of the country's historical experience. Hence, at the national and regional levels, there is an indication of a close positive relationship between urbanization and development.

At the provincial level, multiple regression analyses show that development variables are the main determinants of urbanization. These variables are industrialization and commercialization, farm mechanization, better

communication or higher literacy, urban in-migration from other province
and proximity to the metropolitan area. Demographic factors (child-woma
ratio or fertility and farm density) that denote the rural pressure to migrate seem insignificant (which agrees with findings of other recent studies
Rather than induce permanent migration, better road networks apparently
improve rural-urban interchange, which may be a favorable implication
for rural development.

Internal migration patterns indicate not only long-distance movements
between regions but also transfers from one socioeconomic type of milieu
to another. These transfers more or less follow the regional pattern of
urbanization and development of opportunity. Accordingly, Metro Manila
has been the prime destination of streams from both more urbanized and
less urbanized regions. The frontier regions likewise gained a great deal
from these two sources and experienced much intraregional movements,
not because of their urban but rather because of their agricultural opportunities. In turn, the more urbanized regions also drew migrants, particularly from the less urbanized regions. The less urbanized regions appeared
to be the least attractive to both their own natives or residents and migrants from the other regions. Migration reciprocity between regions increased with time as recent streams became noticeably less effective, i.e.,
counterstreams became appreciably stronger.

Rural-rural migration streams were the most voluminous—about one-
third of all intersectoral lifetime migration—followed by rural-urban
streams (at some 30 percent). During the 1965-1973 period, both types
of streams reduced their relative magnitudes to one-fifth and one-fourth,
respectively, as the other streams became more prominent. As with the
interregional streams, there was greater mutuality or interchange between
urban areas and the metro area, and even between these areas, on the one
hand, and the rural environs, on the other. Thus, net rural-urban and rural
metro transfers together accounted for 31 and 25 percent, respectively,
of the total volume of lifetime and recent migrations. This means a dimin
ishing net effectiveness of migration on permanent rural-urban population
transfers.

An analysis of the characteristics of the different migration streams
shows that rural-urban migration seems to be more a positive than a negative contribution to the development process. This is because migrants
are positively selected and selection tends to be more intense the more
urbanized and developed is the area of destination. As a consequence,

migrants have a fair chance for success (as indicated by education and income) at the place of settlement. Thus, migrants to the metropolitan area are superior to migrants going elsewhere, and those destined to more urbanized areas are better off than migrants to less urbanized or rural areas. In-migrants are, on the average, as well off as native urbanites or metropolitanites. In some cases, recent in-migrants appear inferior to natives, but in time they can be on the same level as, or even superior to, the natives. In all cases, migrants from less urbanized or rural areas are significantly superior to those who stay behind, a clear indication that rural-urban migration is a positive move, at least for the migrants themselves.

Finally, a prospective projection indicates the level of urbanization (proportion urban) to be about 47 percent by 2000 A.D. Urban population would be some 37 million and rural population would number approximately 42 million (on the basis of the medium variant total population projection). The level of citification (proportion in cities of 100,000 or more) would be roughly 32 percent, and the population in cities would be around 25 million. Of these city residents, 62 percent or about 16 million may be concentrated in Metro Manila.

CONCLUSIONS AND IMPLICATIONS

The study findings are essentially in accord with our initial hypotheses. Interestingly, they tend to run counter to popular conclusions about urbanization in developing countries. These beliefs seem to have evolved from erroneous notions of urbanization, as well as from a failure to view urbanization in a broad framework that includes population growth, development, and migration. For instance, what is referred to as rapid urbanization appears to be the unabated concentration of population in the primate city, so that massive rural-urban migration is considered to be synonymous with the influx into the metropolis.[1] These may be the perceptions primarily of metropolitan residents (which include the researcher, the planner, and the policy-maker) who are incessantly harassed by the nuisances of traffic, crimes, floods, slums, and urban eyesores.

An approach to the subject of urbanization based on these narrow notions is misleading and could be counterproductive with respect to the development objective, if development is accepted as socioeconomic transformation and not merely gross increases in output. For it tends to ignore the large rural majority, or even worse, both rural and urban populations outside the metropolitan city. These populations need improvement more than those in the metro area both because of their sheer numbers and the long tradition of neglect by the central government.

It is more correct to conceive of urbanization as a transformation of the population from rural to urban as mirrored in the rise of the proportion urban. As such, it is a process that involves the urban population outside the metropolitan area as well as the predominant rural population This view seems to be more appropriate for purposes of national and regional development planning to the extent that the urban and the rural sectors, in addition to the metropolitan, can be considered within the broad national system.

Based on this study, some implications for policy and further research can be pointed out. First, it must be accepted that what is to be confront is not rapid but unbalanced urbanization. The phenomenon of primacy whereby national urbanization is concentrated in Metro Manila and dilute elsewhere must be understood as the cumulative consequence of historica economic and demographic trends, engendered by the long tradition of interest in the metropolis and neglect elsewhere, as well as the supremacy long given to efficiency over equity. A desire to "nationalize" urbanization by spreading it to the other regions would therefore entail a redefinition of basic concepts, interests, and priorities.

Second, it must be recognized that the change in level of urbanization can be effected essentially by three factors: rural natural increase (which either dampens the rise in urban proportion or promotes reclassification of places), urban natural increase, and rural-urban migration. While it may be desirable, and even imperative, to arrest the first two, it may not be feasible to turn back the third factor to the extent that it forms an integra part of the development process itself. A slowing-down of natural reproduction in both rural and urban sectors may allow for more manageable and wholesome rural-urban shifts. It would be more manageable in that the amount of transfers would be proportionately greater relative to both rural and urban growth but smaller in absolute terms than otherwise. It would be more wholesome in that the shifts would perhaps be more in line with mopping up excess labor from the rural sector for absorption in the urban sector, or vice versa.

Third, the urban sector must be viewed as a system that also includes cities and urban areas outside the metro region. In this context, the national urban pattern may be refashioned by channeling potential metro-bound migratory flows into other urban centers (perhaps the designated regional urban centers). In addition, potential metro out-migrants may be guided to these other centers. Our analysis has shown that migration streams have become less unidirectional and increasingly multidirectional, suggesting that the preconditions for the management of migration traffic may already exist. One of the policy instruments for this management might be to set up *migration guidance offices* in the various regions from which potential migrants can seek information and advice on destinations or on the costs and benefits of migration. Such offices might be linked to the newly established public information offices for jobs of the Department of Labor and regional offices of the National Economic and Development Authority and the National Housing Authority. However, there is need for more research into the feasibility of this management concept, including the specific tools to effect it; for example, a survey on people's space perceptions or "mental maps," their attitudes toward certain destination areas or cities, and how they tend to practice migration vis-à-vis their perceptions and attitudes (see, e.g., Fuller and Chapman, 1974; Fuguitt and Zuiches, 1975).

Fourth, the finding in this study (also supported by other studies) that important determinants of rural-urban population shifts are economic development factors in both sectors rather than demographic pressure in rural areas suggests that rural development may not and should not be considered as an antidote to urbanization. Rather, it implies that rural development, along with a purposive industrial location strategy, can be a major contribution to a policy of balanced urbanization. The government has already established a strategy for industrial dispersal which requires new industries to locate outside the 50-kilometer radius from the center of Manila. This strategy seems short-sighted, however, for provinces peripheral to the metropolitan ring have already been benefiting, and the ring is just going to expand faster to form a megalopolis.[2] Less urbanized and frontier regions, as identified in this study, should be given special consideration for the location of industries, perhaps those of the resource-oriented type.[3]

Fifth, if the desire is indeed to spread and "nationalize" urbanization and development, then a population distribution policy should be made explicit, firm, and consistent. This policy should be accorded adequate emphasis and support—for example, like that given the national family planning program which seems to be *the* population policy. More importantly, it should be framed in consideration of other policies and program explicit or implicit, that are likely to impinge directly or indirectly on population movements. Clearly, an intelligent distribution policy should be formulated and implemented, at least in coordination with the rural development policy, regional development policy, industrial dispersal strategy, and plans for the metropolitan region. Research is needed to anticipate the intended and unintended effects on spatial mobility of different development programs and projects. For instance, national development plans have claimed a pursuit for regional development (Republic of the Philippines, 1973). But this does not seem to have enough vigor, as development projects in the regions continue to be overshadowed and effectively offset by gigantic investments, both public and private, in the metropolis (e.g., the building of the "New City" on reclaimed portions of Manila Bay, and the frenetic construction of hotels and shopping centers in congested areas of the city).

Finally, this analysis of migrants' characteristics corroborates the findings of other studies that migration is a positive move for the migrants themselves. Still to be determined are the impact on areas of origin and destination or what happens to the sending and receiving communities. For instance, it is quite likely that, because rural-urban migrants are positively selected, the rural community stands to lose its "agents of change" instead of being eased of excess "bodies."

NOTES

1. This view has led to an apparent contradiction, namely, that the country has been urbanizing *rapidly* and yet is *predominantly* rural, and will continue to be so for some time.

2. For an elaboration of the concept of the megalopolis, see Gottman (1961).

3. A number of studies have shown that a determined and consistent industrial location policy can be an effective vehicle for redesigning urbanization patterns. For example, Russia was able to shift urban growth from east to west in this manner (Lewis, et al., 1974); similarly did Israel and Eastern Bloc countries (Brutzkus, 1975 In India, a more balanced urban growth has been made possible by means of a consistent decentralization policy (Jacobson and Prakash, 1968). Population redistribution in Brazil in the 1960s was generally consonant with the government's policy to encourage frontier growth (Yoder and Fuguitt, 1974). An extreme case seems to be that of Cuba for which it is reported that urbanization was slowed down by reversing migration streams from urban to rural areas in mid-1960s (Acosta and Hardoy, 1972).

APPENDIX

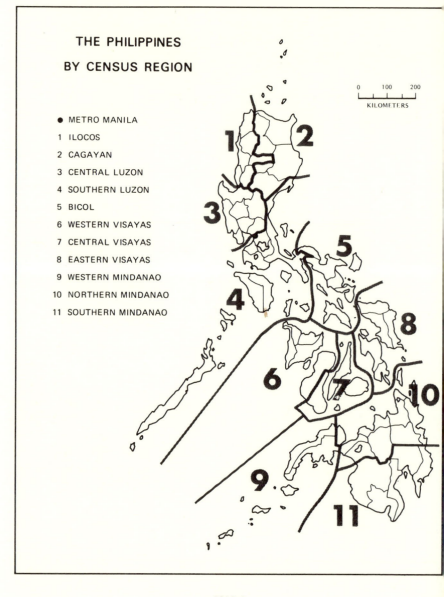

THE PHILIPPINES
BY CENSUS REGION

- METRO MANILA
1 ILOCOS
2 CAGAYAN
3 CENTRAL LUZON
4 SOUTHERN LUZON
5 BICOL
6 WESTERN VISAYAS
7 CENTRAL VISAYAS
8 EASTERN VISAYAS
9 WESTERN MINDANAO
10 NORTHERN MINDANAO
11 SOUTHERN MINDANAO

0   100   200
KILOMETERS

MAP 2

TABLE 1

Philippines: Components of Urban Growth at National, Regional, and Provincial Levels, 1903-1939

Region/Province	Net Reclassification	Percent	Natural Increase	Percent	Net Migration	Percent	Urban Growth (100 pct.)
PHILIPPINES	1,659,739	67.7	875,161	35.7	−84,406	−3.4	2,450,494
Metro Manila	219,300	33.9	356,029	55.1	71,255	11.0	646,584
I. Ilocos	62,038	93.1	67,711	101.6	−63,090	−94.6	66,659
Abra	0	0.0	2,799	105.3	−141	−5.3	2,658
Ilocos Norte	0	0.0	48,386	−3,166.6	−49,914	3,266.6	−1,528
Ilocos Sur	4,281	55.1	16,526	212.6	−13,035	−167.7	7,772
La Union	5,431	100.0	0	0.0	0	0.0	5,431
Mt. Province	6,580	100.0	0	0.0	0	0.0	6,580
Benguet	45,746	100.0	0	0.0	0	0.0	45,746
II. Cagayan Valley	50,466	69.6	7,694	10.6	14,307	19.7	72,467
Batanes	0	0.0	0	0.0	0	0.0	0
Cagayan	19,361	54.5	5,063	14.2	11,134	31.3	35,558
Isabela	16,960	100.0	0	0.0	0	0.0	16,960
Neuva Vizcaya	8,828	60.3	2,631	18.0	3,173	21.7	14,632
Kalinga-Apayao	2,722	100.0	0	0.0	0	0.0	2,722
Ifugao	2,595	100.0	0	0.0	0	0.0	2,595

TABLE 1 (cont.)

Region/Province	Net Reclassification	Percent	Natural Increase	Percent	Net Migration	Percent	Urban Growth (100 pct.)
III. Central Luzon	204,939	85.8	85,500	35.8	-51,672	-21.6	238,767
Bataan	12,038	55.6	15,873	73.3	-6,254	-28.9	21,657
Bulacan	27,807	95.6	656	2.3	615	2.1	29,078
Nueva Ecija	62,944	100.3	12,062	19.2	-12,235	-19.5	62,771
Pampanga	23,224	107.5	7,344	34.0	-8,959	-41.5	21,609
Pangasinan	54,075	82.9	21,719	33.3	-10,603	-16.3	65,191
Tarlac	17,662	61.7	17,219	60.2	-6,275	-21.9	28,606
Zambales	7,189	72.9	10,627	107.8	-7,961	-80.8	9,855
IV. Southern Tagalog	176,449	75.5	69,432	29.7	-12,273	-5.3	233,608
Batangas	15,494	58.5	20,559	77.7	-9,578	-36.2	26,475
Cavite	63,979	91.2	10,937	15.6	-4,778	-6.8	70,138
Laguna	17,997	50.9	19,004	53.8	-1,668	-4.7	35,333
Marinduque	7,408	100.0	0	0.0	0	0.0	7,408
Occ. Mindoro	2,688	100.0	0	0.0	0	0.0	2,688
Or. Mindoro	4,373	100.0	0	0.0	0	0.0	4,373
Palawan	1,356	100.0	0	0.0	0	0.0	1,356
Quezon	40,243	70.8	12,277	21.6	4,294	7.6	56,814
Rizal	19,445	76.1	6,656	26.0	-544	-2.1	25,557
Romblon	3,466	100.0	0	0.0	0	0.0	3,466
V. Bicol	128,388	85.2	63,943	42.5	-41,766	-27.7	150,565
Albay	23,787	64.7	22,450	61.1	-9,480	-25.8	36,757
Camarines Norte	24,755	89.0	1,988	7.1	1,064	3.8	27,807
Camarines Sur	15,090	152.5	20,276	204.9	25,470	-257.4	9,896

Catanduanes	15,766	81.6	3,418	17.7	127	0.7	19,311
Masbate	26,236	100.0	0	0.0	0	0.0	26,236
Sorsogon	22,754	74.5	15,811	51.7	−8,007	−26.2	30,558
VI. Western Visayas	232,847	71.9	109,283	33.7	−18,175	−5.6	323,955
Aklan	764	74.3	4,847	471.0	−4,582	−445.3	1,029
Antique	4,149	85.7	7,149	147.7	−6,457	−133.4	4,841
Capiz	3,241	51.8	5,562	88.9	−2,544	−40.6	6,259
Iloilo	46,034	50.8	63,447	70.1	−18,927	−20.9	90,554
Negros Occ.	178,659	80.7	28,279	12.8	14,334	6.5	221,272
VII. Central Visayas	123,985	60.7	44,289	21.7	36,024	17.6	204,298
Bohol	15,145	100.0	0	0.0	0	0.0	15,145
Cebu	62,372	44.1	38,205	27.0	40,706	28.8	141,283
Negros Oriental	46,468	97.1	6,083	12.7	−4,681	−9.8	47,870
VIII. Eastern Visayas	133,428	81.9	45,812	28.1	−16,331	−10.0	162,909
Leyte / Southern Leyte	63,481	69.9	30,550	33.7	−3,245	−3.6	90,786
Eastern Samar / Northern Samar / Western Samar	69,947	97.0	15,262	21.2	−13,086	−18.1	72,123
IX. Western Mindanao	111,801	90.5	5,572	4.5	6,232	5.0	123,605
Sulu	25,997	100.0	0	0.0	0	0.0	25,997
Zamboanga del Nte.	33,259	92.7	3,033	8.5	−417	−1.2	35,875
Zamboanga del Sur	52,548	85.1	2,539	4.1	6,649	10.8	61,733
X. Northern Mindanao	112,167	91.1	19,896	16.2	−8,917	−7.2	123,146
Agusan del Norte / Agusan del Sur	7,625	83.1	2,932	31.9	−1,377	−15.0	9,180
Bukidnon	0	0.0	0	0.0	0	0.0	0
Lanao del Sur	11,814	102.5	2,223	19.3	−2,515	−21.8	11,522

TABLE 1 (cont.)

Region/Province	Net Reclassification	Percent	Natural Increase	Percent	Net Migration	Percent	Urban Growth (100 pct.)
Lanao del Norte	0	0.0	0	0.0	0	0.0	0
Misamis Occ.	26,616	94.5	2,204	7.8	−648	−2.3	28,172
Misamis Or.	17,695	72.1	4,807	19.6	2,046	8.3	24,548
Surigao del Norte } Surigao del Sur	48,417	97.4	7,731	15.5	−6,424	−12.9	49,724
Camiguin	0	0.0	0	0.0	0	0.0	0
XI. Southern							
Mindanao	103,931	0.0	0	0.0	0	0.0	103,931
Cotabato } South Cotabato	39,803	0.0	0	0.0	0		39,803
Davao del Sur } Davao del Nte. } Davao Oriental	64,128	0.0	0	0.0	0		64,128

Note: Appendix Tables 1 through 9 were derived by applying the procedures spelled out in Chapter 3 to census data (various years). See also the Annex for Chapter 3 for the derivation of metropolitan, urban, and rural rates of natural increase (used with the census data) from the 1973 NDS.

TABLE 2

Philippines: Components of Urban Growth at National, Regional, and Provincial Levels, 1939-1960

Region/Province	Net Reclassification	Percent	Natural Increase	Percent	Net Migration	Percent	Urban Growth (100 pct.)
PHILIPPINES	2,100,240	45.4	1,805,444	39.1	716,130	15.5	4,621,814
Metro Manila	137,272	9.0	666,571	43.8	719,332	47.2	1,523,175
I. Ilocos	31,839	43.9	68,140	93.6	-27,142	-37.3	72,837
Abra	0	0.0	3,295	248.1	-1,967	-148.1	1,328
Ilocos Norte	-6,914	104.0	25,716	-386.9	-25,448	382.9	-6,646
Ilocos Sur	5,095	53.4	72,842	134.5	-8,387	-87.8	9,550
La Union	24,126	89.1	2,853	10.5	99	0.4	27,078
Mt. Province	3,608	116.3	3,456	111.4	-3,963	-127.8	3,101
Benguet	5,924	15.4	19,978	52.0	12,524	32.6	38,426
II. Cagayan Valley	78,943	90.3	33,854	38.7	-25,380	-29.0	87,417
Batanes	0	0.0	0	0.0	0	0.0	0
Cagayan	12,215	82.8	15,694	106.4	-13,164	-89.3	14,745
Isabela	46,770	106.9	7,326	16.7	-10,348	-23.7	43,748
Nueva Vizcaya	16,251	65.5	9,471	38.2	-929	-3.7	24,793
Kalinga-Apayao	656	100.0	0	0.0	0	0.0	656
Ifugao	3,051	87.8	1,363	39.2	-939	-27.0	3,475
III. Central Luzon	476,356	82.2	153,365	26.5	-50,329	-8.7	579,392
Bataan	-21,969	118.2	9,003	-48.4	-5,618	30.2	-18,584
Bulacan	55,730	89.0	11,037	17.6	-4,115	-6.6	62,652
Nueva Ecija	38,329	48.3	38,402	48.4	2,659	3.3	79,390
Pampanga	161,167	94.7	16,632	9.8	-7,559	-4.4	170,240
Pangasinan	139,068	75.5	47,144	25.6	-1,960	-1.1	184,252

TABLE 2 (cont.)

Region/Province	Net Reclassification	Percent	Natural Increase	Percent	Net Migration	Percent	Urban Growth (100 pct.)
Tarlac	59,421	122.8	22,088	45.7	-33,129	-68.5	48,380
Zambales	44,610	84.1	9,059	17.1	-607	-1.1	53,062
IV. Southern Tagalog	304,325	60.4	165,751	32.9	33,635	6.7	503,711
Batangas	21,018	42.3	27,858	56.1	802	1.6	49,678
Cavite	56,401	53.7	41,098	39.1	7,580	7.2	105,079
Laguna	76,248	58.5	29,136	22.3	25,051	19.2	130,435
Marinduque	0	0.0	3,891	300.2	-2,595	-200.2	1,296
Occ. Mindoro	6,766	89.4	1,412	18.7	-607	-8.0	7,571
Or. Mindoro	29,174	100.7	2,297	7.9	-2,490	-8.6	28,981
Palawan	17,182	91.1	2,124	11.3	-436	-2.3	18,870
Quezon	62,405	59.0	38,173	36.1	5,144	4.9	105,722
Rizal	32,722	60.8	17,941	33.4	3,131	5.8	53,794
Romblon	2,409	105.4	1,821	79.7	-1,945	-85.1	2,285
V. Bicol	148,841	54.3	105,783	38.6	19,650	7.2	274,276
Albay	535	2.8	28,754	151.9	-10,358	-54.7	18,931
Camarines Norte	-114	-0.7	11,872	74.0	4,276	26.7	16,034
Camarines Sur	120,584	69.2	19,631	11.3	34,109	19.6	174,324
Catanduanes	6,496	57.6	12,463	110.5	-7,676	-68.0	11,283
Masbate	17,421	58.4	6,184	20.7	6,226	20.9	29,831
Sorsogon	3,919	16.4	26,879	112.6	-6,927	-29.0	23,871
VI. Western Visayas	228,789	48.7	225,340	47.9	15,971	3.4	470,100
Aklan	-764	-75.3	3,428	337.7	-1,649	-162.5	1,015
Antique	-2,829	-356.7	6,571	828.6	-2,949	-371.9	793
Capiz	7,917	59.9	6,325	47.8	-1,015	-7.7	13,227
Iloilo	10,482	14.9	90,621	128.7	-30,668	-43.5	70,435
Negros Occ.	213,983	55.6	118,296	30.8	52,251	13.6	384,630

VII. Central Visayas	146,112	50.0	122,436	41.9	23,661	8.1	292,209
Bohol	9,540	50.5	7,955	42.1	1,404	7.4	18,899
Cebu	90,472	42.3	90,325	42.2	33,248	15.5	214,045
Negros Oriental	46,100	77.8	24,155	40.8	-10,990	-18.5	59,265
VIII. Eastern Visayas	91,257	56.7	105,790	65.8	-36,224	-22.5	160,823
Leyte / Southern Leyte	51,311	51.2	63,147	63.1	-14,324	-14.3	100,134
Eastern Samar / Northern Samar / Western Samar	39,946	65.8	42,643	70.3	-21,900	-36.1	60,689
IX. Western Mindanao	58,113	60.9	46,852	49.1	-9,504	-10.0	95,461
Sulu	29,822	105.4	10,614	37.5	-12,134	-42.9	28,302
Zamboanga del Nte.	-4,975	-76.5	11,185	172.0	292	4.5	6,502
Zamboanga del Sur	33,266	54.8	25,054	41.3	2,337	3.9	60,657
X. Northern Mindanao	202,943	75.7	67,341	25.1	-2,338	-0.9	267,946
Agusan del Norte / Agusan del Sur	26,052	51.9	6,812	13.6	17,298	34.5	50,162
Bukidnon	30,950	100.0	0	0.0	0	0.0	30,950
Lanao del Norte	22,392	53.9	7,340	17.7	11,781	28.4	41,513
Lanao del Sur	89,222	100.0	0	0.0	0	0.0	89,222
Misamis Occ.	-2,669	58.1	11,023	-239.8	-12,950	281.8	-4,596
Misamis Or.	34,524	63.1	17,524	32.0	2,695	4.9	54,743
Surigao del Norte / Surigao del Sur	2,472	41.5	24,643	414.0	-21,163	-355.6	5,952
Camiguin	0	0.0	0	0.0	0	0.0	0
XI. Southern Mindanao	195,450	66.4	44,221	15.0	54,798	18.6	294,469
Cotabato / South Cotabato	106,285	78.2	18,995	14.0	10,704	7.9	135,984
Davao del Norte / Davao del Sur / Davao Oriental	89,165	56.3	25,225	15.9	44,095	27.8	158,485

TABLE 3

Philippines: Components of Urban Growth at National, Regional, and Provincial Levels, 1960-1970

Region/Province		Net Reclassification	Percent	Natural Increase	Percent	Net Migration	Percent	Urban Growth (100 pct.)
PHILIPPINES		1,125,235	28.2	2,165,797	54.2	705,284	17.6	3,996,316
Metro Manila		124,815	8.2	829,377	54.3	571,935	37.5	1,526,127
I.	Ilocos	51,159	50.9	56,341	56.1	−7,082	−7.1	100,418
	Abra	0	0.0	2,140	71.0	873	29.0	3,013
	Ilocos Norte	15,513	50.3	14,566	47.2	754	2.4	30,833
	Ilocos Sur	17,594	88.3	10,761	54.0	−8,439	−42.4	19,916
	La Union	10,602	94.9	6,069	54.3	−5,500	−49.2	11,171
	Mt. Province	−6,440	95.4	912	−13.5	−1,223	18.1	−6,751
	Benguet	13,890	32.9	21,893	51.8	6,453	15.3	42,236
II.	Cagayan	11,424	15.8	38,021	52.5	22,992	31.7	72,437
	Batanes	0	0.0	0	0.0	0	0.0	0
	Cagayan	7,513	36.4	14,428	69.9	−1,295	−6.3	20,646
	Isabela	8,083	18.0	13,531	30.1	23,306	51.9	44,920
	Nueva Vizcaya	−6,258	−293.7	8,251	387.2	138	6.5	2,131
	Kalinga-Apayao	0	0.0	951	52.1	875	47.9	1,826
	Ifugao	2,086	71.6	859	29.5	−31	−1.1	2,914

III.	Central Luzon	342,145	55.6	222,898	36.2	50,092	8.1	615,135
	Bataan	21,307	73.0	5,779	19.8	2,108	7.2	29,194
	Bulacan	206,338	91.3	25,123	11.1	−5,534	−2.4	225,927
	Nueva Ecija	18,092	34.5	42,655	81.4	−8,331	−15.9	52,416
	Pampanga	76,341	42.3	51,083	28.3	53,174	29.4	180,598
	Pangasinan	−17,241	−41.7	58,734	142.0	−123	−0.3	41,370
	Tarlac	−17,889	−5,454.0	17,945	5,471.0	272	82.9	328
	Zambales	55,197	64.7	21,580	25.3	8,525	10.0	85,302
IV.	Southern Tagalog	342,787	52.5	221,318	33.9	88,653	13.6	652,758
	Batangas	43,581	76.3	26,729	46.8	−13,183	−23.1	57,127
	Cavite	18,212	19.5	52,220	55.9	23,015	24.6	93,447
	Laguna	114,545	60.1	50,661	26.6	25,455	13.4	190,661
	Marinduque	2,229	56.7	2,451	62.4	−752	−19.1	3,928
	Occ. Mindoro	14,448	59.6	2,888	11.9	6,895	28.5	24,231
	Or. Mindoro	9,562	43.5	8,304	37.8	4,102	18.7	21,968
	Palawan	2,381	26.1	4,550	49.9	2,180	23.9	9,111
	Quezon	42,689	45.0	47,134	49.7	4,995	5.3	94,818
	Rizal	95,140	60.9	24,762	15.9	36,284	23.2	156,186
	Romblon	0	0.0	1,619	126.4	−338	−26.4	1,281
V.	Bicol	82,659	64.1	125,478	97.3	−79,118	−61.3	129,019
	Albay	43,294	79.1	22,981	42.0	−11,528	−21.1	54,747
	Camarines Norte	5,783	37.1	13,067	83.8	−3,262	−20.9	15,588
	Camarines Sur	25,485	109.9	47,299	204.0	−49,601	−214.0	23,183
	Catanduanes	−4,343	147.4	8,634	−293.1	−7,237	245.7	2,946
	Masbate	5,855	36.5	11,637	72.6	1,454	−9.1	16,038
	Sorsogon	6,585	29.4	21,860	97.6	−6,036	−26.9	22,409

TABLE 3 (cont.)

	Net Reclassification	Percent	Natural Increase	Percent	Net Migration	Percent	Urban Growth (100 pct.)
VI. Western Visayas	−146,860	−245.6	193,818	324.1	12,842	21.5	59,800
Aklan	9,249	71.0	2,339	18.0	1,437	11.0	13,025
Antique	11,134	66.6	4,901	29.3	685	4.1	16,720
Capiz	31,597	85.8	7,509	20.4	−2,265	−6.1	36,841
Iloilo	10,347	12.5	68,405	82.9	3,746	4.5	82,498
Negros Occ.	−209,187	234.3	110,663	−123.9	9,240	−10.3	−89,284
VII. Central Visayas	152,756	50.3	138,965	45.7	12,146	4.0	303,867
Bohol	13,435	65.2	8,060	39.1	−896	−4.3	20,599
Cebu	149,212	52.8	105,719	37.4	27,611	9.8	282,542
Negros Oriental	−9,891	−1,362.4	25,186	3,469.1	−14,569	−2,006.7	726
VIII. Eastern Visayas	4,222	6.4	95,640	144.3	−33,601	−50.7	66,261
Leyte ⎰ Southern Leyte	−4,920	−13.7	54,812	152.1	−13,852	−38.4	36,040
Eastern Samar ⎱ Northern Samar Western Samar	9,142	30.3	40,828	135.1	−19,749	−65.3	30,221
IX. Western Mindanao	30,803	40.8	51,947	68.7	−7,147	−9.5	75,603
Sulu	13,244	47.4	14,462	51.8	221	0.8	27,927

Zamboanga del Sur	9,328	23.6	26,104	66.1	4,078	10.3	39,510
X. Northern Mindanao	42,542	31.4	88,602	65.3	4,495	3.3	135,639
Agusan del Norte	13,956	25.7	14,447	26.6	25,932	47.1	54,335
Agusan del Sur	25,222	96.4	2,516	9.6	−1,586	−6.1	26,152
Bukidnon	11,370	60.0	5,915	31.2	1,653	8.7	18,938
Lanao del Norte	−14,501	65.8	9,097	−41.3	−16,628	75.5	−22,032
Lanao del Sur	−4,182	−18.7	17,667	79.2	8,833	39.6	22,318
Misamis Occ.	6,918	74.5	7,099	76.4	−4,727	−50.9	9,290
Misamis Or.	−5,479	56.5	15,691	161.9	−520	−5.4	9,692
Surigao del Norte Surigao del Sur	9,238	54.5	16,170	95.4	−8,462	−49.9	16,946
Camiguin	0	0.0	0	0.0	0	0.0	0
XI. Southern Mindanao	86,783	33.5	103,392	39.9	69,077	26.6	259,252
Cotabato Southern Cotabato	52,221	46.2	43,008	38.0	17,828	15.8	113,057
Davao del Norte Davao del Sur Davao Oriental	34,562	23.6	60,384	41.3	51,249	35.1	146,195

TABLE 4

Philippines: Components of the Net Reclassification Portion of Urban Growth
at National, Regional, and Provincial Levels, 1903-1939

Region/Province	Basic Rural Population	Percent	Natural Increase	Percent	Net Migration	Percent	Net Reclassification (100 pct.)
PHILIPPINES	511,726	30.8	636,562	38.4	511,451	30.8	1,659,739
Metro Manila	33,248	15.2	41,359	18.9	144,693	66.0	219,300
I. Ilocos	6,160	9.9	7,663	12.4	48,215	77.7	62,038
Abra	0	0.0	0	0.0	0	0.0	0
Ilocos Norte	0	0.0	0	0.0	0	0.0	0
Ilocos Sur	3,681	86.0	4,579	107.0	−3,979	−92.9	4,281
La Union	1,972	36.3	2,453	45.2	1,006	18.5	5,431
Mt. Province	0	0.0	0	0.0	6,580	100.0	6,580
Benguet	507	1.1	631	1.4	44,608	97.5	45,746
II. Cagayan Valley	17,445	34.6	21,701	43.0	11,320	22.4	50,466
Batanes	0	0.0	0	0.0	0	0.0	0
Cagayan	9,198	47.5	11,442	59.1	−1,279	−6.6	19,361
Isabela	3,991	23.5	4,965	29.3	8,004	47.2	16,960
Nueva Vizcaya	4,256	48.2	5,294	60.0	−722	−8.2	8,828
Kalinga-Apayao	0	0.0	0	0.0	2,722	100.0	2,722
Ifugao	0	0.0	0	0.0	2,595	100.0	2,595

III.	Central Luzon	108,855	53.1	135,410	66.1	−39,326	−19.2	204,939
	Bataan	6,436	53.5	8,006	66.5	−2,404	−20.0	12,038
	Bulacan	14,574	52.4	18,129	65.2	−4,896	−17.6	27,807
	Nueva Ecija	21,683	34.4	26,973	42.9	14,288	22.7	62,944
	Pampanga	14,170	61.0	17,627	75.9	−8,573	−36.9	23,224
	Pangasinan	35,517	65.7	44,181	81.7	−25,623	−47.4	54,075
	Tarlac	9,529	54.0	11,854	67.1	−3,721	−21.1	17,662
	Zambales	6,946	96.6	8,640	120.2	−8,397	−116.8	77,189
IV.	Southern Tagalog	82,749	46.9	102,936	58.3	−9,236	−5.2	176,449
	Batangas	9,588	61.9	11,927	77.0	−6,021	−38.9	15,494
	Cavite	19,019	29.7	23,659	37.0	21,301	33.3	63,979
	Laguna	11,861	65.9	14,755	82.0	−8,619	−47.9	17,997
	Marinduque	3,769	50.9	4,688	63.3	−1,049	−14.2	7,408
	Occ. Mindoro	2,010	74.8	2,500	93.0	−1,822	−67.8	2,688
	Or. Mindoro	1,294	29.6	1,610	36.8	1,469	33.6	4,373
	Palawan	603	44.5	750	55.3	3	0.2	1,356
	Quezon	20,482	50.9	25,479	63.3	−5,718	−14.2	40,243
	Rizal	11,770	60.5	14,641	75.3	−6,966	−35.8	19,445
	Romblon	2,353	67.9	2,927	84.4	−1,814	−52.3	3,466
V.	Bicol	44,247	34.5	55,041	42.9	29,100	22.7	128,388
	Albay	9,565	40.2	11,898	50.0	2,324	9.8	23,787
	Camarines Norte	3,613	14.6	4,494	18.2	16,648	67.3	24,755
	Camarines Sur	10,351	68.6	12,876	85.3	−8,137	−53.9	15,090
	Catanduanes	7,957	50.5	9,898	62.8	−2,089	−13.3	15,766
	Masbate	5,044	19.2	6,274	23.9	14,918	56.9	26,236
	Sorsogon	7,717	33.9	9,600	42.2	5,437	23.9	22,754

TABLE 4 (cont.)

Region/Province	Basic Rural Population	Percent	Natural Increase	Percent	Net Migration	Percent	Net Reclassification (100 pct.)
VI. Western Visayas	60,017	25.8	74,658	32.1	98,172	42.2	232,847
Aklan	446	58.4	555	72.6	−237	−31.0	764
Antique	4,993	120.3	6,211	149.7	−7,055	−170.0	4,149
Capiz	2,883	89.0	3,586	110.6	−3,228	−99.6	3,241
Iloilo	12,283	26.7	15,279	33.2	18,472	40.1	46,034
Negros Occ.	39,412	22.1	49,027	27.4	90,220	50.5	178,659
VII. Central Visayas	52,869	42.6	65,766	53.0	5,350	4.3	123,985
Bohol	6,845	45.2	8,515	56.2	−215	−1.4	15,145
Cebu	32,443	52.0	40,358	64.7	−10,429	−16.7	62,372
Negros Oriental	13,581	29.2	16,894	36.4	15,993	34.4	46,468
VIII. Eastern Visayas	44,113	33.1	54,874	41.1	34,441	25.8	133,428
Leyte / Southern Leyte	19,400	30.6	24,133	38.0	19,948	31.4	63,481
Eastern Samar / Northern Samar / Western Samar	24,713	35.3	30,742	44.0	14,492	20.7	69,947
IX. Western Mindanao	12,354	11.0	15,368	13.7	84,079	75.2	111,801
Sulu	1,270	4.9	1,580	6.1	23,147	89.0	25,997
Zamboanga del Nte.	3,253	9.8	4,047	12.2	25,959	78.1	33,259
Zamboanga del ...	7,8??	11.0	9,741	19.5	24,972	66.6	52,545

X. Northern Mindanao	40,000	41.0	37,220	5_._	6,_ _ _	_._	112,_ _ _
Agusan del Norte ⎫ Agusan del Sur ⎭	2,057	27.0	2,559	33.6	3,009	39.5	7,626
Bukidnon	0	0.0	0	0.0	0	0.0	0
Lanao del Norte	0	0.0	0	0.0	11,814	100.0	11,814
Lanao del Sur	0	0.0	0	0.0	0	0.0	0
Misamis Occ.	6,952	26.1	8,648	32.5	11,016	41.4	26,616
Misamis Or.	8,900	50.3	11,071	62.6	-2,276	-12.9	17,695
Camiguin	0	0.0	0	0.0	0	0.0	0
Surigao del Nte. ⎫ Surigao del Sur ⎭	28,096	58.0	34,950	72.2	-14,629	-30.2	48,417
XI. Southern Mindanao	3,664	3.5	4,558	4.4	95,709	92.1	103,931
Cotabato ⎫ South Cotabato ⎭	1,051	2.6	1,307	3.3	37,445	94.1	39,803
Davao del Norte ⎫ Davao del Sur ⎪ Davao Oriental ⎭	2,613	4.1	3,250	5.1	58,265	90.0	64,128

TABLE 5

Philippines: Components of the Net Reclassification Portion of Urban Growth at National,
Regional, and Provincial Levels, 1939-1960

Region/Province	Basic Rural Population	Percent	Natural Increase	Percent	Net Migration	Percent	Net Reclassification (100 pct.)
PHILIPPINES	1,004,334	47.8	771,722	36.7	324,184	15.4	2,100,240
Metro Manila	47,840	34.9	36,760	26.8	52,672	38.4	137,272
I. Ilocos	37,295	117.1	28,657	90.0	−34,113	−107.1	31,839
Abra	0	0.0	0	0.0	0	0.0	0
Ilocos Norte	3,129	−45.3	2,404	−34.8	−12,447	180.0	−6,914
Ilocos Sur	8,196	160.9	6,298	123.6	−9,399	−184.5	5,095
La Union	11,799	48.9	9,066	37.6	3,261	13.5	24,126
Mt. Province	1,764	48.9	1,355	37.6	489	13.6	3,608
Benguet	12,407	209.4	9,533	160.9	−16,016	−270.4	5,924
II. Cagayan Valley	32,007	40.5	24,594	31.2	22,342	28.3	78,943
Batanes	0	0.0	0	0.0	0	0.0	0
Cagayan	16,449	134.7	12,639	103.5	−16,873	−138.1	12,215
Isabela	8,777	18.8	6,744	14.4	31,249	66.8	46,770
Nueva Vizcaya	5,156	31.7	3,962	24.4	7,133	43.9	16,251
Kalinga-Apayao	597	91.0	459	70.0	−400	−61.0	656
Ifugao	1,028	33.7	790	25.9	1,233	40.4	3,051

Bataan	1,593	−7.3	1,224	−5.6	−24,786	112.8	−21,969
Bulacan	35,790	64.2	27,501	49.3	−7,561	−13.6	55,730
Nueva Ecija	19,109	49.9	14,683	38.3	4,537	11.8	38,329
Pampanga	60,553	37.6	46,528	28.9	54,086	33.6	161,167
Pangasinan	85,070	61.2	65,367	47.0	−11,369	−8.2	139,068
Tarlac	16,564	27.9	12,728	21.4	30,129	50.7	59,421
Zambales	12,910	28.9	9,920	22.2	21,780	48.8	44,610
IV. Southern Tagalog	140,689	46.2	108,243	35.6	55,213	18.1	304,325
Batangas	9,541	45.4	7,331	34.9	4,146	19.7	21,018
Cavite	34,757	61.6	26,707	47.4	−5,063	−9.0	56,401
Laguna	37,301	48.9	28,662	37.6	10,285	13.5	76,248
Marinduque	0	0.0	0	0.0	0	0.0	0
Occ. Mindoro	2,036	30.1	1,564	23.1	3,166	46.8	6,766
Or. Mindoro	11,204	38.4	8,609	29.5	9,361	32.1	29,174
Palawan	12,006	69.9	9,225	53.7	−4,049	−23.6	17,182
Quezon	26,143	41.9	20,088	32.2	16,174	25.9	62,405
Rizal	6,250	10.1	4,802	14.7	21,670	66.2	32,722
Romblon	1,631	67.7	1,253	52.0	−475	−19.7	2,409
V. Bicol	81,199	54.6	62,393	41.9	5,249	3.5	148,841
Albay	6,573	1,228.6	5,051	944.1	−11,089	−2,072.7	535
Camarines Nte.	2,738	−2,401.8	2,104	−1,845.6	−4,956	4,347.4	−114
Camarines Sur	47,181	39.1	36,253	30.1	37,150	30.8	120,584
Catanduanes	4,234	65.2	3,253	50.1	−991	−15.3	6,496
Masbate	17,230	98.9	13,239	76.0	−13,048	−74.9	17,421
Sorsogon	3,243	82.8	2,492	63.6	−1,816	−46.3	3,919

TABLE 5 (cont.)

Region/Province	Basic Rural Population	Percent	Natural Increase	Percent	Net Migration	Percent	Net Reclassification (100 pct.)
VI. Western Visayas	125,225	54.7	96,222	42.1	7,342	3.2	228,789
Aklan	0	0.0	0	0.0	-764	100.0	-764
Antique	2,278	-80.5	1,750	-61.9	-6,857	242.4	-2,829
Capiz	2,340	29.6	1,798	22.7	3,779	47.7	7,917
Iloilo	6,958	66.4	5,346	51.0	-1,822	-17.4	10,482
Negros Occ.	113,649	53.1	87,327	40.8	13,007	6.1	213,983
VII. Central Visayas	65,338	44.7	50,205	34.4	30,569	20.9	146,112
Bohol	5,751	60.3	4,419	46.3	-630	-6.6	9,540
Cebu	54,174	59.9	41,627	46.0	-5,329	-5.9	90,472
Negros Oriental	5,413	11.7	4,159	9.0	36,528	79.2	46,100
VIII. Eastern Visayas	64,129	70.3	49,276	54.0	-22,148	-24.3	91,257
Leyte Southern Leyte	30,928	60.3	23,765	46.3	-3,382	-6.6	51,311
Eastern Samar Northern Samar Western Samar	33,201	83.1	25,511	63.9	-18,766	-47.0	39,946
IX. Western Mindanao	39,709	68.3	30,512	52.5	-12,108	-20.8	58,113
Sulu	8,810	29.5	6,770	22.7	14,242	47.8	29,822
Zamboanga del Nte.	18,524	372.3	14,234	286.1	-37,733	-758.5	-4,975
Zamboanga del Sur	12,375	27.2	9,509	28.6	11,...	...	...

X.	Northern Mindanao	80,996	39.9	62,237	30.7	59,710	29.4	202,943
	Agusan del Norte ⎫ Agusan del Sur ⎬	9,353	35.9	7,187	27.6	9,512	36.5	26,052
	Bukidnon	7,979	25.8	6,131	19.8	16,840	54.4	30,950
	Lanao del Norte	10,031	44.8	7,708	34.4	4,653	20.8	22,392
	Lanao del Sur	22,644	25.4	17,399	19.5	49,179	55.1	89,222
	Misamis Occ.	5,359	−200.8	4,118	−154.3	−12,146	455.1	−2,669
	Misamis Or.	14,667	42.5	11,270	32.6	8,587	24.9	34,524
	Camiguin	–	–	–	–	–	–	–
	Surigao del Norte ⎫ Surigao del Sur ⎬	10,963	443.5	8,424	340.8	−16,915	−684.3	2,472
XI.	Southern Mindanao	58,138	29.7	44,673	22.9	92,639	47.4	195,450
	Cotabato ⎫ South Cotabato ⎬	10,942	10.3	8,408	7.9	86,935	81.8	106,285
	Davao del Norte ⎫ Davao del Sur ⎬ Davao Oriental ⎭	47,196	52.9	36,265	40.7	5,704	6.4	89,165

TABLE 6

Philippines: Components of the Net Reclassification Portion of Urban Growth
at National, Regional, and Provincial Levels, 1960-1970

Region/Province	Basic Rural Population	Percent	Natural Increase	Percent	Net Migration	Percent	Net Reclassification (100 pct.)
PHILIPPINES	1,006,769	89.5	388,215	34.5	−269,749	−24.0	1,125,235
Metro Manila	41,736	33.4	16,094	12.9	66,985	53.7	124,815
I. Ilocos	44,288	86.6	17,078	33.4	−10,207	−20.0	51,159
Abra	0	0.0	0	0.0	0	0.0	0
Ilocos Norte	1,401	9.0	540	3.5	13,572	87.5	15,513
Ilocos Sur	17,119	97.3	6,601	37.5	−6,126	−34.8	17,594
La Union	13,506	127.4	5,208	49.1	−8,112	−76.5	10,602
Mt. Province	0	0.0	0	0.0	−6,440	100.0	−6,440
Benguet	12,262	88.3	4,728	34.0	−3,100	−22.3	13,890
II. Cagayan Valley	20,998	183.8	8,097	70.9	−17,671	−154.7	11,424
Batanes	0	0.0	0	0.0	0	0.0	0
Cagayan	7,973	106.1	3,074	40.9	−3,534	−47.0	7,513
Isabela	5,312	65.7	2,048	25.3	723	8.9	8,083
Nueva Vizcaya	4,585	−73.3	1,768	−28.3	−12,611	201.5	−6,258
Kalinga-Apayao	0	0.0	0	0.0	0	0.0	0
Ifugao	3,128	150.0	1,206	57.8	−2,248	−107.8	2,086
III. Central Luzon	254,562	74.4	98,160	28.7	−10,577	−3.1	342,145
Bataan	16,112	75.6	6,213	29.2	−1,018	−4.8	21,307
Bulacan	128,987	62.5	49,738	24.1	27,613	13.4	206,338
Nueva Ecija	20,705	114.4	7,984	44.1	−10,597	−58.6	18,092
Pampanga	43,286	56.7	16,691	21.9	16,364	21.4	76,341
Pangasinan	31,971	−185.4	12,328	−71.5	−61,540	356.9	−17,241

	Tarlac	8,814	-49.3	3,399	-19.0	-30,102	168.3	-17,889
	Zambales	4,687	8.5	1,807	3.3	48,703	88.2	55,197
IV.	Southern Tagalog	210,701	61.5	81,247	23.7	50,839	14.8	342,787
	Batangas	27,897	64.0	10,757	24.7	4,927	11.3	43,581
	Cavite	7,358	40.4	2,837	15.6	8,017	44.0	18,212
	Laguna	82,645	72.2	31,868	27.8	32	0.0	114,545
	Marinduque	1,943	87.2	749	33.6	-463	-20.8	2,229
	Occ. Mindoro	6,706	46.4	2,586	17.9	5,156	35.7	14,448
	Or. Mindoro	6,303	65.9	2,430	25.4	829	8.7	9,562
	Palawan	4,317	181.3	1,665	69.9	-3,601	-151.2	2,381
	Quezon	34,480	80.8	13,296	31.1	-5,087	-11.9	42,689
	Rizal	39,052	41.0	15,059	15.8	41,029	43.1	95,140
	Romblon	0	0.0	0	0.0	0	0.0	0
V.	Bicol	61,666	74.6	23,779	28.8	-2,786	-3.4	82,659
	Albay	14,124	32.6	5,446	12.6	23,724	54.8	43,294
	Camarines Nte.	2,016	34.9	777	13.4	2,990	51.7	5,783
	Camarines Sur	28,202	110.7	10,875	42.7	-13,592	-53.3	25,485
	Catanduanes	0	0.0	0	0.0	-4,343	100.0	-4,343
	Masbate	14,566	248.8	5,617	95.9	-14,328	244.7	5,855
	Sorsogon	2,758	41.9	1,063	16.1	2,764	42.0	6,585
VI.	Western Visayas	56,921	-38.8	21,949	-14.9	-225,730	153.7	-146,860
	Aklan	6,933	75.0	2,673	28.9	-357	-3.9	9,249
	Antique	6,673	59.9	2,573	23.1	1,888	17.0	11,134
	Capiz	18,161	57.5	7,003	22.2	6,433	20.4	31,597
	Iloilo	8,735	84.4	3,368	32.6	-1,756	-17.0	10,347
	Negros Occ.	16,419	-7.8	6,331	-3.0	-231,937	110.9	-209,187
VII.	Central Visayas	116,583	76.3	44,955	29.4	-8,782	-5.7	152,756
	Bohol	16,723	124.5	6,448	48.0	-9,736	-72.5	13,435
	Cebu	88,940	59.6	34,296	23.0	25,976	17.4	149,212
	Negros Or.	10,920	-110.4	4,211	-42.6	-25,022	253.0	-9,891

TABLE 6 (cont.)

Region/Province	Basic Rural Population	Percent	Natural Increase	Percent	Net Migration	Percent	Net Reclassification (100 pct.)
VIII. Eastern Visayas	19,198	454.7	7,403	175.3	−22,379	−530.1	4,222
Leyte Southern Leyte	11,221	−228.1	4,327	−87.9	−20,468	416.0	−4,920
Eastern Samar Northern Samar Western Samar	7,977	87.3	3,076	33.6	−1,911	−20.9	9,142
IX. Western Mindanao	23,386	75.9	9,018	29.3	−1,601	−5.2	30,803
Sulu	5,494	41.5	2,119	16.0	5,631	42.5	13,244
Zamboanga del Nte.	8,393	102.0	3,236	39.3	−3,398	−41.3	8,231
Zamboanga del Sur	9,499	101.8	3,663	39.3	−3,834	−41.1	9,328
X. Northern Mindanao	88,887	208.9	34,275	80.6	−80,620	−189.5	42,542
Agusan del Norte	7,795	55.9	3,006	21.5	3,155	22.6	13,956
Agusan del Sur	11,220	44.5	4,326	17.2	9,676	38.4	25,222
Bukidnon	11,241	98.9	4,335	38.1	−4,206	−37.0	11,370
Lanao del Norte	7,940	−54.8	3,062	−21.1	−25,503	175.9	−14,501
Lanao del Sur	17,486	−418.1	6,743	−161.2	−28,411	679.4	−4,182
Misamis Occ.	6,414	92.7	2,473	35.7	−1,969	−28.5	6,918
Misamis Or.	12,636	−230.6	4,873	−88.9	−22,988	419.6	−5,479
Camiguin	0	0.0	0	0.0	0	0.0	0
Surigao del Norte Surigao del Sur	14,155	153.2	5,458	59.1	−10,375	−112.3	9,238
XI. Southern Mindanao	67,843	78.2	26,161	30.1	−7,221	−8.3	86,783
Cotabato South Cotabato	42,374	81.1	16,340	31.3	−6,493	−12.4	52,221
Davao del Norte Davao del Sur Davao Oriental	25,469	73.7	9,821	28.4	−728	−2.1	34,562

TABLE 7

Philippines: Aggregated Components of Urban Growth at National, Regional, and Provincial Levels, 1903-1939

Region/Province	Basic Rural Population	Percent	Aggregate NI	Percent	Aggregate Net Migration	Percent	Total (100 pct.)
PHILIPPINES	511,726	20.9	1,511,723	61.7	427,045	17.4	2,450,494
Metro Manila	33,248	5.1	397,388	61.5	215,948	33.4	646,584
I. Ilocos	6,160	9.2	75,374	113.1	-14,875	-22.3	66,659
Abra	0	0.0	2,799	105.3	-141	-5.3	2,658
Ilocos Norte	0	0.0	48,386	-3,166.6	-49,914	3,266.6	-1,528
Ilocos Sur	3,681	47.4	21,105	271.6	-17,014	-219.0	7,772
La Union	1,972	36.3	2,453	45.2	1,006	18.5	5,431
Mt. Province	0	0.0	0	0.0	6,580	100.0	6,580
Benguet	507	1.1	631	1.4	44,608	97.5	45,746
II. Cagayan Valley	17,445	24.1	29,395	40.6	25,627	35.4	72,467
Batanes	0	0.0	0	0.0	0	0.0	0
Cagayan	9,198	25.9	16,505	46.4	9,855	27.7	35,558
Isabela	3,991	23.5	4,965	29.3	8,004	47.2	16,960
Nueva Vizcaya	4,256	29.1	7,925	54.2	2,451	16.8	14,632
Kalinga-Apayao	0	0.0	0	0.0	2,722	100.0	2,722
Ifugao	0	0.0	0	0.0	2,595	100.0	2,595
III. Central Luzon	108,855	45.6	220,910	92.5	-90,998	-38.1	238,767
Bataan	6,436	29.7	23,879	110.3	-8,658	-40.0	21,657
Bulacan	14,574	50.1	18,785	64.6	-4,281	-14.7	29,078
Nueva Ecija	21,683	34.5	39,035	62.2	2,053	3.3	62,771
Pampanga	14,170	65.6	24,971	115.6	-17,532	-81.1	21,609
Pangasinan	35,517	54.5	65,900	101.1	-36,226	-55.6	65,191

TABLE 7 (cont.)

Region/Province	Basic Rural Population	Percent	Aggregate NI	Percent	Aggregate Net Migration	Percent	Total (100 pct.)
Tarlac	9,529	33.3	29,073	101.6	-9,996	-34.9	28,606
Zambales	6,946	70.5	19,267	195.5	-16,358	-166.0	9,855
IV. Southern Tagalog	82,749	35.4	172,368	73.8	-21,509	-9.2	233,608
Batangas	9,588	36.2	32,486	122.7	-15,599	-58.9	26,475
Cavite	19,019	27.1	34,596	49.3	16,523	23.6	70,138
Laguna	11,861	33.6	33,759	95.5	-10,287	-29.1	35,333
Marinduque	3,769	50.9	4,688	63.3	-1,049	-14.2	7,408
Occ. Mindoro	2,010	74.8	2,500	93.0	-1,822	-67.8	2,688
Or. Mindoro	1,294	29.6	1,610	36.8	1,469	33.6	4,373
Palawan	603	44.5	750	55.3	3	0.2	1,356
Quezon	20,482	36.1	37,756	66.5	-1,424	-2.5	56,814
Rizal	11,770	46.1	21,297	83.3	-7,510	-29.4	25,557
Romblon	2,353	67.9	2,927	84.4	-1,814	-52.3	3,466
V. Bicol	44,247	29.4	118,984	79.0	-12,666	-8.4	150,565
Albay	9,565	26.0	34,348	93.4	-7,156	-19.5	36,757
Camarines Norte	3,613	13.0	6,482	23.3	17,712	63.7	27,807
Camarines Sur	10,351	104.6	33,152	335.0	-33,607	-339.6	9,896
Catanduanes	7,957	41.2	13,316	69.0	-1,962	-10.2	19,311
Masbate	5,044	19.2	6,274	23.9	14,918	56.9	26,236
Sorsogon	7,717	25.3	25,411	83.2	-2,570	-8.4	30,558
VI. Western Visayas	60,017	18.5	183,941	56.8	79,997	24.7	323,955
Aklan	446	43.3	5,402	525.0	-4,819	-468.3	1,029
Antique	4,993	103.1	13,360	276.0	-13,512	-279.1	4,841
Capiz	2,883	46.1	9,148	146.2	-5,772	-92.2	6,259
Iloilo	12,283	13.6	78,726	86.9	-455	-0.5	90,554

VII. Central Visayas	52,869	25.9	110,055	53.3	4,374	25.0	251,228
Bohol	6,845	45.2	8,515	56.2	−215	−1.4	15,145
Cebu	32,443	23.0	78,563	55.6	30,277	21.4	141,283
Negros Oriental	13,581	28.4	22,977	48.0	11,312	23.6	47,870
VIII. Eastern Visayas	44,113	27.1	100,686	61.8	18,110	11.1	162,909
Leyte / Southern Leyte	19,400	21.4	54,683	60.2	16,703	18.4	90,786
Eastern Samar / Northern Samar / Western Samar	24,713	34.3	46,004	63.8	1,406	1.9	72,123
IX. Western Mindanao	12,354	10.0	20,940	16.9	90,311	73.1	123,605
Sulu	1,270	4.9	1,580	6.1	23,147	89.0	25,997
Zamboanga del Norte	3,253	9.1	7,080	19.7	25,542	71.2	35,875
Zamboanga del Sur	7,831	12.7	12,280	19.9	41,622	67.4	61,733
X. Northern Mindanao	46,005	37.4	77,124	62.6	17	0.0	123,146
Agusan del Norte / Agusan del Sur	2,057	22.4	5,491	59.8	1,632	17.8	9,180
Bukidnon	0	0.0	0	0.0	0	0.0	0
Lanao del Sur	0	0.0	2,223	19.3	9,299	80.7	11,522
Lanao del Norte	0	0.0	0	0.0	0	0.0	0
Misamis Occ.	6,952	24.7	10,852	38.5	10,368	36.8	28,172
Misamis Or.	8,900	36.3	15,878	64.7	−230	−0.9	24,548
Surigao del Norte	28,096	56.5	42,681	85.8	−21,053	−42.3	49,724
Surigao del Sur / Camiguin	0	0.0	0	0.0	0	0.0	0
XI. Southern Mindanao	3,664	3.5	4,558	4.4	95,709	92.1	103,931
Cotabato / South Cotabato	1,051	2.6	1,307	3.3	37,445	94.1	39,803
Davao del Sur / Davao del Norte / Davao Oriental	2,613	4.1	3,250	5.1	58,265	90.9	64,128

TABLE 8

Philippines: Aggregated Components of Urban Growth at National, Regional, and Provincial Levels, 1939-1960

Region/Province	Basic Rural Population	Percent	Aggregate NI	Percent	Aggregate Net Migration	Percent	Total (100 pct.)
PHILIPPINES	1,004,334	21.7	2,577,166	55.8	1,040,314	22.5	4,621,814
Metro Manila	47,840	3.1	703,331	46.2	772,004	50.7	1,523,175
I. Ilocos	37,295	51.2	96,797	132.9	-61,255	-84.1	72,837
Abra	0	0.0	3,295	248.1	-1,967	-148.1	1,328
Ilocos Norte	3,129	-47.1	28,120	-423.1	-37,895	570.2	-6,646
Ilocos Sur	8,196	85.8	19,140	200.4	-17,786	-186.2	9,550
La Union	11,799	43.6	11,919	44.0	3,360	12.4	27,078
Mt. Province	1,764	56.9	4,811	155.1	-3,474	-112.0	3,101
Benguet	12,407	32.3	29,511	76.8	-3,492	-9.1	38,426
II. Cagayan Valley	32,007	36.6	58,448	66.9	-3,038	-3.5	87,417
Batanes	0	0.0	0	0.0	0	0.0	0
Cagayan	16,449	111.6	28,333	192.2	-30,037	-203.7	14,745
Isabela	8,777	20.1	14,070	32.2	20,901	47.8	43,748
Nueva Vizcaya	5,156	20.8	13,433	54.2	6,204	25.0	24,793
Kalinga-Apayao	597	91.0	459	70.0	-400	-61.0	656
Ifugao	1,028	29.6	2,153	62.0	294	8.5	3,475
III. Central Luzon	231,589	40.0	331,316	57.2	16,487	2.8	579,392
Bataan	1,593	-8.6	10,227	-55.0	-30,404	163.6	-18,584
Bulacan	35,790	57.1	38,538	61.5	-11,676	-18.6	62,652
Nueva Ecija	19,109	24.1	53,085	66.9	7,196	9.1	79,390
Pampanga	60,553	35.6	63,160	37.1	46,527	27.3	170,240
Pangasinan	85,070	46.2	112,511	61.1	13,329	-7.2	184,253

Tarlac	48,380	-6.2	-3,000	72.0	34,816	34.2	16,564
Zambales	53,062	39.9	21,173	35.8	18,979	24.3	12,910
IV. Southern Tagalog	503,711	17.6	88,848	54.4	273,994	27.9	140,689
Batangas	49,678	10.0	4,948	70.8	35,189	19.2	9,541
Cavite	105,079	2.4	2,517	64.5	67,805	33.1	34,757
Laguna	130,435	27.1	35,336	44.3	57,798	28.6	37,301
Marinduque	1,296	-200.2	-2,595	300.2	3,891	0.0	0
Occ. Mindoro	7,571	33.8	2,559	39.3	2,976	26.9	2,036
Or. Mindoro	28,981	23.7	6,871	37.6	10,906	38.7	11,204
Palawan	18,870	-23.8	-4,485	60.1	11,349	63.6	12,006
Quezon	105,722	20.2	21,318	55.1	58,261	24.7	26,143
Rizal	53,794	46.1	24,801	42.3	22,743	11.6	6,250
Romblon	2,285	-105.9	-2,420	134.5	3,074	71.4	1,631
V. Bicol	274,274	9.1	24,899	61.3	168,176	29.6	81,199
Albay	18,931	-113.3	-21,447	178.6	33,805	34.7	6,573
Camarines Norte	16,034	-4.2	-680	87.2	13,976	17.1	2,738
Camarines Sur	174,324	40.9	71,259	32.1	55,884	27.1	47,181
Catanduanes	11,283	-76.8	-8,667	139.3	15,716	37.5	4,234
Masbate	29,831	-22.9	-6,822	65.1	19,423	57.8	17,230
Sorsogon	23,871	-36.6	-8,743	123.0	29,371	13.6	3,243
VI. Western Visayas	470,100	5.0	23,313	68.4	321,562	26.6	125,225
Aklan	1,015	-237.7	-2,413	337.7	3,428	0.0	0
Antique	793	-1,236.6	-9,806	1,049.3	8,321	287.3	2,278
Capiz	13,227	20.9	2,764	61.4	8,123	17.7	2,340
Iloilo	70,435	-46.1	-32,490	136.2	95,967	9.9	6,958
Negros Occ.	384,630	17.0	65,258	53.5	205,723	29.5	113,649
VII. Central Visayas	292,209	18.6	54,230	59.1	172,641	22.4	65,338
Bohol	18,899	4.1	774	65.5	12,374	30.4	5,751
Cebu	214,045	13.0	27,919	61.6	131,952	25.3	54,174
Negros Oriental	59,265	43.1	25,538	47.8	28,314	9.1	5,413

TABLE 8 (cont.)

Region/Province	Basic Rural Population	Percent	Aggregate NI	Percent	Aggregate Net Migration	Percent	Total (100 pct.)
VIII. Eastern Visayas	64,129	39.9	155,066	96.4	-58,372	-36.3	160,823
Leyte Southern Leyte	30,928	30.9	86,912	86.8	-17,706	-17.7	100,134
Eastern Samar: Northern Samar Western Samar	33,201	54.7	68,154	112.3	-40,666	-67.0	60,689
IX. Western Mindanao	39,709	41.6	77,364	81.0	-21,612	-22.6	95,461
Sulu	8,810	31.1	17,384	61.4	2,108	7.4	28,302
Zamboanga del Nte.	18,524	284.9	25,419	390.9	-37,441	-575.8	6,502
Zamboanga del Sur	12,375	20.4	34,563	57.0	13,719	22.6	60,657
X. Northern Mindanao	80,996	30.2	129,578	48.4	57,372	21.4	267,946
Agusan del Norte Agusan del Sur	9,353	18.6	13,999	27.9	26,810	53.4	50,162
Bukidnon	7,979	25.8	6,131	19.8	16,840	54.4	30,950
Lanao del Norte	10,031	24.2	15,048	36.2	16,434	39.6	41,513
Lanao del Sur	22,644	25.4	17,399	19.5	49,179	55.1	89,222
Misamis Occ.	5,359	-116.6	15,141	-329.4	-25,096	546.0	-4,596
Misamis Or.	14,667	26.8	28,794	52.6	11,282	20.6	54,743
Camiguin	0	0.0	0	0.0	0	0.0	0
Surigao del Norte Surigao del Sur	10,963	184.2	33,067	555.6	-38,078	-639.8	5,952
XI. Southern Mindanao	58,138	19.7	88,894	30.2	147,437	50.1	294,469
Cotabato South Cotabato	10,942	8.0	27,403	20.2	97,639	71.8	135,984
Davao del Norte Davao del Sur Davao Oriental	47,196	29.8	61,490	38.8	49,799	31.4	158,485

TABLE 9

Philippines: Aggregated Components of Urban Growth at National, Regional, and Provincial Levels, 1960-1970

Region/Province	Basic Rural Population	Percent	Aggregate NI	Percent	Aggregate Net Migration	Percent	Total (100 pct.)
PHILIPPINES	1,006,769	25.2	2,554,012	63.9	435,535	10.9	3,996,316
Metro Manila	41,736	2.7	845,471	55.4	638,920	41.9	1,526,127
I. Ilocos	44,288	44.1	73,419	73.1	-17,289	-17.2	100,418
Abra	0	0.0	2,140	71.0	873	29.0	3,013
Ilocos Norte	1,401	4.5	15,106	49.0	14,326	46.5	30,833
Ilocos Sur	17,119	86.0	17,362	87.2	-14,565	-73.1	19,916
La Union	13,506	120.9	11,277	100.9	-13,612	-121.9	11,171
Mt. Province	0	0.0	912	-13.5	-7,663	113.5	-6,751
Benguet	12,262	29.0	26,621	63.0	3,353	7.9	42,236
II. Cagayan Valley	20,998	29.0	46,118	63.7	5,321	7.3	72,437
Batanes	0	0.0	0	0.0	0	0.0	0
Cagayan	7,973	38.6	17,502	84.8	-4,829	-23.4	20,646
Isabela	5,312	11.8	15,579	34.7	24,029	53.5	44,920
Nueva Vizcaya	4,585	215.2	10,019	470.2	-12,473	-585.3	2,131
Kalinga-Apayao	0	0.0	951	52.1	875	47.9	1,826
Ifugao	3,128	107.3	2,065	70.9	-2,279	-78.2	2,914
III. Central Luzon	254,562	41.4	321,058	52.2	39,515	6.4	615,315
Bataan	16,112	55.2	11,992	41.1	1,090	3.7	29,194
Bulacan	128,987	57.1	74,861	33.1	22,079	9.8	225,927
Nueva Ecija	20,705	39.5	50,639	96.6	-18,928	-36.1	52,416
Pampanga	43,286	24.0	67,774	37.5	69,538	38.5	180,598
Pangasinan	31,971	77.3	71,062	171.8	-61,663	-149.1	41,370

TABLE 9 (cont.)

Region/Province	Basic Rural Population	Percent	Aggregate NI	Percent	Aggregate Net Migration	Percent	Total (100 pct.)
Tarlac	8,814	2687.2	21,344	6507.3	−29,830	−9,094.5	328
Zambales	4,687	5.5	23,387	27.4	57,228	67.1	85,302
IV. Southern Tagalog	210,701	32.3	302,565	46.4	139,492	21.4	652,758
Batangas	27,897	48.8	37,486	65.6	−8,256	−14.5	57,127
Cavite	7,358	7.9	55,057	58.9	31,032	33.2	93,447
Laguna	82,645	43.3	82,529	43.3	25,487	13.4	190,661
Marinduque	1,943	49.5	3,200	81.5	−1,215	−30.9	3,928
Occ. Mindoro	6,706	27.7	5,474	22.6	12,051	49.7	24,231
Or. Mindoro	6,303	28.7	10,734	48.9	4,931	22.4	21,968
Palawan	4,317	47.4	6,215	68.2	−1,421	−15.6	9,111
Quezon	34,480	36.4	60,430	63.7	−92	−0.1	94,818
Rizal	39,052	25.0	39,821	25.5	77,313	49.5	156,186
Romblon	0	0.0	1,619	126.4	−338	−26.4	1,281
V. Bicol	61,666	47.8	149,257	115.7	−81,904	−63.5	129,019
Albay	14,124	25.8	28,427	51.9	12,196	22.3	54,747
Camarines Norte	2,016	12.9	13,844	88.8	−272	−1.7	15,588
Camarines Sur	28,202	121.6	58,174	250.9	−63,193	−272.6	23,182
Catanduanes	0	0.0	8,634	−293.1	−11,580	393.1	−2,946
Masbate	14,566	90.8	17,254	107.6	−15,782	−98.4	16,038
Sorsogon	2,758	12.3	22,923	102.3	−3,272	−14.6	22,409
VI. Western Visayas	56,921	95.2	215,767	360.8	−212,888	−356.0	59,800
Aklan	6,933	53.2	5,012	38.5	1,080	8.3	13,025
Antique	6,673	39.9	7,474	44.7	2,573	15.4	16,720
Capiz	18,161	49.3	14,512	39.4	4,168	11.3	36,841
Iloilo	8,735	10.6	71,773	87.0	1,990	2.4	82,498
Negros Occ.	16,419	−18.4	116,994	−131.0	−222,697	249.4	−89,284

VII. Central Visayas	116,583	38.3	183,920	60.5	3,364	1.1	303,867
Bohol	16,723	81.2	14,508	70.4	−10,632	−51.6	20,599
Cebu	88,940	31.5	140,015	49.6	53,587	19.0	282,542
Negros Oriental	10,920	1504.1	29,397	4,049.2	−39,591	−5,453.3	726
VIII. Eastern Visayas	19,198	29.0	103,043	155.5	−55,980	−84.5	66,261
Leyte / Southern Leyte	11,221	31.1	59,139	164.1	−34,320	−95.2	36,040
Eastern Samar / Northern Samar / Western Samar	7,977	26.4	43,904	145.3	−21,660	−71.7	30,221
IX. Western Mindanao	23,386	30.9	60,965	80.6	−8,748	−11.6	75,603
Sulu	5,494	19.7	16,581	59.4	5,852	21.0	27,927
Zamboanga del Nte.	8,393	102.8	14,618	179.0	−14,845	−181.8	8,166
Zamboanga del Sur	9,499	24.0	29,767	75.3	244	0.6	39,510
X. Northern Mindanao	88,887	65.5	122,877	90.6	−76,125	−56.1	135,639
Agusan del Norte	7,795	14.3	17,453	32.1	29,087	53.5	54,335
Agusan del Sur	11,220	42.9	6,842	26.2	8,090	30.9	26,152
Bukidnon	11,241	59.4	10,250	54.1	−2,553	−13.5	18,938
Lanao del Norte	7,940	−36.0	12,159	−55.2	−42,131	191.2	−22,032
Lanao del Sur	17,486	78.3	24,410	109.4	−19,578	−87.7	22,318
Misamis Occ.	6,414	69.0	9,572	103.0	−6,696	−72.1	9,290
Misamis Or.	12,636	130.4	20,564	212.2	−23,508	−242.6	9,692
Camiguin	0	0.0	0	0.0	0	0.0	0
Surigao del Norte / Surigao del Sur	14,155	83.5	21,628	127.6	−18,837	−111.2	16,946
XI. Southern Mindanao	67,843	26.2	129,553	50.0	61,856	23.9	259,252
Cotabato / South Cotabato	42,374	37.5	59,348	52.5	11,335	10.0	113,057
Davao del Norte / Davao del Sur / Davao Oriental	25,469	17.4	70,205	48.0	50,521	34.6	146,195

TABLE 10

Provincial Data on Variables Used in Multiple Regressions

PROVINCE	U_{70}	$U_{70}-\hat{U}_{70}$	MC_{60}	FM_{60}	R_{60}	CWR_{60}	UI_{60-70}	FD_{60}	RN_{60}	PM
1. Abra	7.3	-1.116	1.7	15.3	2.6	844.5	0.476	2615.5	86.6	0
2. Ilocos Norte	24.8	3.876	5.9	31.1	5.3	752.4	0.694	4317.3	166.5	0
3. Ilocos Sur	15.9	1.789	9.5	16.8	5.1	766.8	0.354	3848.7	177.3	0
4. La Union	11.7	-1.292	8.9	55.7	6.8	877.3	0.215	3734.4	210.6	0
5. Mt. Province	24.5	-1.305	10.8	41.4	6.1	779.7	0.429	2034.5	85.0	0
6. Batanes	0.0	0.0	0.0	0.0	2.2	820.1	0.0	2094.4	329.7	0
7. Cagayan	13.3	-1.421	6.1	91.0	2.7	905.2	0.319	1816.4	80.3	0
8. Isabela	16.3	0.664	7.2	88.0	3.2	982.4	0.240	1529.2	52.1	0
9. Nueva Vizcaya	20.3	-12.929	8.0	44.0	3.7	979.0	0.242	2000.0	46.1	0
10. Bataan	24.4	6.221	5.5	68.6	13.0	1016.1	0.223	1576.3	181.4	1
11. Bulacan	55.9	28.976	35.1	61.7	24.4	834.8	2.096	2586.4	179.6	1
12. Nueva Ecija	26.5	-4.085	8.2	116.5	9.3	926.2	0.448	1651.2	158.6	1
13. Pampanga	43.1	6.718	12.3	544.6	16.7	947.6	0.956	2133.5	203.9	1
14. Pangasinan	23.2	-3.826	7.7	67.9	7.4	903.8	0.360	3134.3	205.5	1
15. Tarlac	18.3	-7.709	14.3	80.6	9.4	941.7	0.259	1892.9	185.5	1
16. Zambales	47.2	8.988	9.4	71.3	16.5	860.5	2.550	2599.5	74.8	1
17. Batangas	17.3	0.240	13.5	40.2	10.6	883.6	0.525	2414.0	208.0	1
18. Cavite	54.4	1.748	5.3	66.3	26.2	821.1	1.398	2428.3	292.2	1
19. Laguna	54.7	11.708	9.9	232.0	22.4	935.0	2.113	1718.8	243.6	1
20. Marinduque	8.8	-0.633	1.7	11.4	5.8	1010.6	0.230	1673.8	230.8	1
21. Occidental Mindoro	24.0	9.889	3.6	48.8	5.1	921.7	0.404	684.4	49.6	1
22. Oriental Mindoro	16.9	0.348	3.5	30.6	5.8	1005.3	0.313	1267.8	109.3	1
23. Palawan	13.5	-2.543	4.3	40.3	4.1	875.9	0.279	667.8	31.6	1
24. Quezon	27.8	-1.666	9.5	63.3	10.7	989.1	0.314	1234.0	61.3	1
25. Albay	20.5	2.118	11.5	17.2	4.8	1011.6	0.280	2059.6	208.7	0
26. Camarines Norte	23.7	-3.122	11.2	42.4	7.5	1095.2	0.045	955.4	113.1	0
27. Camarines Sur	25.4	-3.253	7.9	20.8	5.0	1038.6	0.473	1408.3	114.9	0

28. Catanduanes	19.8	−4.683	3.2	1.9	1.9	957.8	0.353	1811.6	195.1	0
29. Masbate	14.6	−4.087	6.5	6.4	3.1	1081.5	0.167	1179.0	97.0	0
30. Sorsogon	23.4	−0.982	2.3	43.8	3.2	1080.5	0.422	1554.4	203.0	0
31. Aklan	8.1	2.633	4.9	9.3	3.0	949.8	0.325	2167.8	150.1	0
32. Antique	11.8	2.672	3.8	19.1	2.7	823.0	0.288	2232.7	139.9	0
33. Capiz	16.1	5.752	5.7	35.8	4.0	996.8	0.251	1999.8	128.9	0
34. Iloilo	27.9	0.671	16.1	74.8	6.4	840.9	0.961	1935.1	216.9	0
35. Negros Occidental	36.8	−13.920	13.6	509.7	5.6	1017.8	0.858	977.2	155.6	0
36. Romblon	4.2	−1.979	3.0	17.2	4.4	1017.3	0.326	1818.8	224.4	0
37. Bohol	8.0	0.499	3.4	6.7	4.9	830.0	0.293	2535.6	355.5	0
38. Cebu	42.2	9.378	27.9	8.6	8.9	848.1	2.615	4081.6	265.2	0
39. Leyte	19.8	−2.141	6.2	24.3	5.5	961.2	0.521	1871.9	135.6	0
40. Negros Oriental	16.7	−5.241	7.2	66.9	3.9	958.8	0.207	2089.7	136.2	0
41. Samar	17.9	−1.702	2.6	12.3	2.6	979.0	0.749	1443.8	56.6	0
42. Agusan	38.0	12.601	17.7	28.4	5.3	968.1	0.445	1171.7	32.2	0
43. Bukidnon	12.0	−5.873	3.6	150.3	4.3	1014.3	0.158	753.9	48.5	0
44. Lanao del Norte	10.5	−13.272	8.1	4.0	6.4	942.6	0.125	1685.5	55.8	0
45. Lanao del Sur	24.5	−1.204	2.9	18.1	1.4	836.7	1.451	1314.6	54.6	0
46. Misamis Occidental	12.0	−1.501	14.5	40.0	7.4	937.9	0.362	1863.9	196.3	0
47. Misamis Oriental	19.6	−5.189	21.7	27.7	9.0	1024.0	0.359	1462.7	88.0	0
48. Surigao	22.5	1.474	5.3	12.7	3.4	882.8	0.641	1391.5	66.1	0
49. Cotabato	18.0	−1.094	8.8	208.2	3.3	970.9	0.345	1064.2	43.9	0
50. Davao	25.2	−2.233	18.0	53.6	8.2	1035.3	0.387	1187.9	38.5	0
51. Sulu	19.3	0.715	3.1	19.0	1.8	858.9	3.860	1544.5	120.0	0
52. Zamboanga del Norte	13.3	−5.082	5.3	17.7	2.9	1039.8	0.234	1298.7	69.4	0
53. Zamboanga del Sur	16.0	−2.890	13.8	25.6	5.0	1046.8	0.242	1175.3	45.7	0

Note: For different notations, see Chapter 4.

SOURCES: Economic Census of the Philippines (1960), Vol. III, Manufacturing: Table 31, and Vol. VI, Commerce: Table 6; Agriculture Census (1960), Vol. I, Reports by Province; Census on Population and Housing (1960), Vols. I and II; Bureau of Public Highways, Annual Report for FY 1960, pp. 109-110; and Census on Population and Housing (1970), Reports by Province.

TABLE 11

Education: Interregional Migrants, 1965-1973, by Sex
(percent distribution)

Type of Stream	None	Elementary 1-4	Elementary 5-7	High School Vocational	College or Above	No Information	Total (100 pct.)
Both Sexes							
More Urban-Metro	0.9	9.2	26.8	36.1	26.3	0.8	303,589
More Urban-Frontier	6.6	31.4	27.5	22.5	11.0	1.0	196,092
Less Urban-Metro	2.1	9.8	36.6	29.0	22.2	0.3	206,194
Less Urban-More Urban	4.5	21.6	40.7	17.7	13.5	2.0	78,440
Less Urban-Frontier	14.4	29.2	26.3	16.7	12.7	0.7	56,866
Frontier-Metro	0.0	0.9	24.0	44.8	29.4	0.9	49,584
All	5.2	16.4	28.1	29.4	20.3	0.6	2,989,817
Males							
More Urban-Metro	0.9	7.0	17.7	39.7	33.3	1.4	118,429
More Urban-Frontier	7.5	22.8	31.3	22.8	14.2	1.4	98,979
Less Urban-Metro	0.6	9.2	25.8	28.0	36.4	0.0	73,254
Less Urban-More Urban	8.3	25.5	39.6	9.3	14.0	3.4	30,436
Less Urban-Frontier	20.5	31.8	18.7	18.7	8.8	1.5	27,136
Frontier-Metro	0.0	0.0	18.6	50.9	28.2	2.3	18,517
All	5.3	17.7	24.4	29.7	22.0	0.8	1,315,744

				Females			
More Urban-Metro	0.9	10.5	32.7	33.8	21.7	0.4	185,160
More Urban-Frontier	5.5	40.3	23.7	22.3	7.7	0.5	97,113
Less Urban-Metro	2.9	10.1	42.6	29.6	14.4	0.5	132,940
Less Urban-More Urban	2.2	19.2	41.4	23.0	13.2	1.1	48,004
Less Urban-Frontier	8.8	26.8	33.1	15.0	16.2	0.0	29,730
Frontier-Metro	0.0	1.5	27.1	41.3	30.1	0.0	31,067
All	5.1	15.3	31.1	29.2	18.8	0.4	1,674,073

Note: The total number of migrants in the six dominant streams do not add up to the number of migrants in *all* sixteen possible streams.

SOURCE: 1973 NDS.

TABLE 12

Education: Interregional Migrants, Birth-1965, by Sex
(percent distribution)

Type of Stream	None	Elementary 1-4	Elementary 5-7	High School Vocational	College or Above	No Information	Total (100 pct.)
				Both Sexes			
More Urban-Metro	2.6	12.3	20.7	32.0	31.6	0.8	486,527
More Urban-Frontier	15.0	34.3	26.6	16.6	6.7	0.7	1,061,933
Less Urban-Metro	2.0	10.7	31.0	31.7	23.4	1.3	232,852
Less Urban-More Urban	5.4	25.4	28.6	27.0	11.5	2.2	198,903
Less Urban-Frontier	11.2	30.0	34.3	13.1	11.5	0.0	226,160
Frontier-Metro	0.0	0.0	29.9	33.6	36.6	0.0	16,095
All	9.1	24.7	26.6	23.4	15.6	0.7	4,787,027
				Males			
More Urban-Metro	1.2	8.4	18.2	33.3	37.9	1.1	233,127
More Urban-Frontier	15.0	34.7	24.6	15.9	9.1	0.6	558,534
Less Urban-Metro	1.5	6.5	23.3	35.4	31.9	1.4	101,401
Less Urban-More Urban	7.2	22.8	30.3	25.2	13.8	0.7	97,116
Less Urban-Frontier	12.8	28.5	37.3	11.8	9.6	0.0	114,828
Frontier-Metro	2.9	0.0	22.2	35.2	36.9	2.8	16,243
All	8.3	24.2	25.4	24.4	17.1	0.7	2,323,348

				Females			
More Urban-Metro	3.9	16.0	22.9	30.9	25.8	0.5	253,400
More Urban-Frontier	15.1	33.9	28.7	17.4	4.0	0.8	503,399
Less Urban-Metro	2.4	13.8	36.9	28.8	16.8	1.2	131,451
Less Urban-More Urban	3.6	27.8	26.9	28.8	9.2	3.7	101,787
Less Urban-Frontier	9.6	31.4	31.2	14.4	13.4	0.0	111,332
Frontier-Metro	2.8	14.8	18.9	27.2	36.3	0.0	16,629
All	9.8	25.3	27.8	22.4	14.2	0.6	2,463,679

Note: The total number of migrants in the six dominant streams do not add up to the number of migrants in *all* sixteen possible streams.

SOURCE: 1973 NDS.

TABLE 13

Education: Nonmigrants by Type of Region, 1973, by Sex
(percent distribution)

Type of Region	None	Elementary 1-4	Elementary 5-7	High School Vocational	College or Above	No Information	Total (100 pct.)
				Both Sexes			
Metropolitan	2.9	6.5	15.7	42.4	31.5	0.9	928,091
More Urbanized	9.1	27.5	28.6	22.6	11.1	1.2	7,591,664
Less Urbanized	11.8	26.1	37.3	16.4	8.0	0.3	2,893,229
Frontier	17.9	21.8	27.1	23.8	8.2	1.2	2,937,771
All	11.1	24.7	29.2	22.9	11.2	1.0	14,350,755
				Males			
Metropolitan	2.3	4.4	15.3	45.7	31.1	1.2	458,276
More Urbanized	7.9	27.4	27.4	26.1	10.0	1.2	3,732,199
Less Urbanized	10.2	25.8	39.2	17.5	7.1	0.2	1,464,747
Frontier	16.2	22.4	28.1	25.0	7.4	0.9	1,459,925
All	9.7	24.6	29.2	25.4	10.2	0.9	7,115,147
				Females			
Metropolitan	3.6	8.6	16.0	39.3	31.8	0.6	469,815
More Urbanized	10.3	27.5	29.7	19.2	12.1	1.2	3,859,465
Less Urbanized	13.5	26.5	35.4	15.2	9.0	0.4	1,428,482
Frontier	19.4	21.3	26.1	22.6	9.0	1.6	1,477,846
All	12.4	24.8	29.2	20.4	12.1	1.1	7,235,608

SOURCE: 1973 NDS

TABLE 14

Cash Income: Interregional Migrants, 1965-1973, by Sex
(percent distribution)

Type of Stream	<1,000	1,000-2,999	3,000-4,999	5,000+	No Information	Total (100 pct.)
			Both Sexes			
More Urban-Metro	65.2	17.2	8.2	5.6	3.7	255,554
More Urban-Frontier	81.2	9.3	4.2	1.3	4.0	180,825
Less Urban-Metro	70.3	18.2	5.3	1.5	4.7	174,659
Less Urban-More Urban	76.3	14.2	3.0	1.0	5.6	65,519
Less Urban-Frontier	75.1	8.4	7.6	3.3	5.6	49,470
Frontier-Metro	62.2	18.8	8.6	6.9	3.5	35,788
All	66.3	16.7	8.4	4.7	4.0	2,653,704
			Males			
More Urban-Metro	44.2	27.7	12.5	11.0	4.7	97,975
More Urban-Frontier	70.8	14.4	6.9	2.4	5.4	92,925
Less Urban-Metro	42.8	39.1	10.1	4.4	3.5	59,867
Less Urban-More Urban	49.2	32.6	7.1	2.4	8.6	27,174
Less Urban-Frontier	65.8	16.5	6.5	5.6	5.7	24,894
Frontier-Metro	21.8	43.0	18.0	11.8	5.3	14,598
All	46.0	28.9	11.6	8.6	4.9	1,207,466

TABLE 14 (cont.)

Type of Stream	<1,000	1,000-2,999	3,000-4,999	5,000+	No Information	Total (100 pct.)
			Females			
More Urban-Metro	78.3	10.7	5.6	2.3	3.1	157,579
More Urban-Frontier	92.2	4.0	1.2	0.0	2.6	87,900
Less Urban-Metro	84.7	7.3	2.8	0.0	5.3	114,792
Less Urban-More Urban	95.5	1.1	0.0	0.0	3.4	38,345
Less Urban-Frontier	84.5	0.1	8.7	1.1	5.5	24,576
Frontier-Metro	90.1	2.1	2.1	3.6	2.2	21,140
All	83.2	6.5	5.7	1.5	3.1	1,446,238

Note: The total number of migrants in the six dominant streams do not add up to the number of migrants in *all* sixteen possible streams.

SOURCE: 1973 NDS.

TABLE 15

Cash Income: Interregional Migrants, Birth-1965, by Sex
(percent distribution)

Type of Stream	<1,000	1,000-2,999	3,000-4,999	5,000+	No Information	Total (100 pct.)
			Both Sexes			
More Urban-Metro	43.1	24.5	14.8	15.1	2.5	431,495
More Urban-Frontier	72.9	18.4	5.1	1.9	1.6	1,001,413
Less Urban-Metro	44.9	22.9	17.2	11.5	3.5	209,769
Less Urban-More Urban	60.6	20.0	12.7	3.8	3.0	180,604
Less Urban-Frontier	66.5	17.3	9.6	3.9	2.7	212,625
Frontier-Metro	26.8	35.5	15.4	12.3	10.0	12,334
All	61.9	21.3	9.3	5.3	2.2	4,348,435
			Males			
More Urban-Metro	14.2	36.2	21.9	25.5	2.2	209,277
More Urban-Frontier	57.2	29.6	7.4	3.3	2.5	544,178
Less Urban-Metro	13.4	34.0	30.0	18.9	3.8	91,250
Less Urban-More Urban	33.8	35.7	18.2	7.8	4.6	88,028
Less Urban-Frontier	51.4	26.9	12.3	6.3	3.1	110,214
Frontier-Metro	6.2	58.1	15.5	20.1	0.0	7,528
All	41.7	33.9	12.9	8.7	2.8	2,151,731

TABLE 15 (cont.)

Type of Stream	<1,000	1,000-2,999	3,000-4,999	5,000+	No Information	Total (100 pct.)
			Females			
More Urban-Metro	70.4	13.4	0.0	5.2	2.7	222,218
More Urban-Frontier	91.5	5.2	0.0	0.2	0.6	457,235
Less Urban-Metro	69.1	14.3	0.0	5.9	3.4	118,519
Less Urban-More Urban	86.2	5.0	0.0	0.0	1.4	92,576
Less Urban-Frontier	82.8	7.1	0.0	1.2	2.3	102,411
Frontier-Metro	59.0	0.0	15.3	0.0	25.7	4,806
All	81.6	8.9	0.0	1.9	1.7	2,196,704

Note: The total number of migrants in the six dominant streams do not add up to the number of migrants in *all* sixteen possible streams.

SOURCE: 1973 NDS.

TABLE 16

Cash Income: Nonmigrants by Type of Region, 1973, by Sex
(percent distribution)

Type of Region	<1,000	1,000-2,999	3,000-4,999	5,000+	No Information	Total (100 pct.)
Both Sexes						
Metropolitan	55.1	19.3	13.2	7.7	4.7	753,118
More Urbanized	70.2	18.2	5.5	1.8	4.3	6,382,919
Less Urbanized	77.6	15.3	4.0	0.9	2.2	2,543,871
Frontier	75.8	14.9	4.0	2.6	2.7	2,505,363
All	72.0	17.0	5.4	2.1	3.6	12,185,271
Males						
Metropolitan	42.6	25.8	15.4	11.2	4.9	379,705
More Urbanized	55.3	29.6	6.5	2.6	5.9	3,223,199
Less Urbanized	67.3	23.7	4.5	1.5	3.0	1,340,320
Frontier	62.6	24.0	5.0	4.3	4.2	1,331,533
All	58.7	26.9	6.3	3.3	4.8	6,274,757
Females						
Metropolitan	67.8	12.6	10.9	4.1	4.6	373,413
More Urbanized	85.4	6.6	4.5	0.9	2.7	3,159,720
Less Urbanized	89.1	5.9	3.4	0.3	1.4	1,203,551
Frontier	90.7	4.7	2.8	0.6	1.1	1,173,830
All	86.1	6.4	4.3	0.9	2.2	5,910,514

SOURCE: 1973 NDS.

TABLE 17

Age Distribution by Sex for Intersectoral Migrants, 1965-1973
(percent distribution)

Type of Stream	15-24	25-34	35-49	50+	Total (100 pct.)
			Both Sexes		
Rural-Rural	39.9	23.4	23.4	13.2	590,594
Rural-Urban	44.7	26.3	19.8	9.2	770,988
Rural-Manila	62.4	18.3	12.3	7.0	405,361
Urban-Urban	33.3	34.4	25.6	6.7	256,196
Urban-Manila	38.8	28.7	20.9	11.6	500,068
Urban-Rural	31.3	35.8	20.6	12.2	335,093
Manila-Rural	40.8	41.2	13.8	4.2	138,518
All	42.5	27.5	20.0	10.0	2,996,818
			Males		
Rural-Rural	37.9	25.3	21.8	14.9	296,503
Rural-Urban	34.7	29.0	24.0	12.4	309,474
Rural-Manila	60.6	20.0	12.6	6.8	153,449
Urban-Urban	24.8	36.6	30.2	8.3	117,120
Urban-Manila	34.9	29.5	22.8	12.8	219,253
Urban-Rural	25.2	37.5	24.9	12.4	158,845
Manila-Rural	37.8	39.9	17.1	5.2	66,269
All	36.6	29.5	22.3	11.6	1,320,913
			Females		
Rural-Rural	41.9	21.5	25.0	11.5	294,091
Rural-Urban	51.4	24.4	17.1	7.1	461,514
Rural-Manila	63.5	17.2	12.0	7.2	251,912
Urban-Urban	40.5	32.6	21.7	5.3	139,076
Urban-Manila	41.9	28.0	19.5	10.6	280,815
Urban-Rural	36.8	34.4	16.7	12.1	176,248
Manila-Rural	43.6	42.3	10.7	3.4	72,249
All	47.2	25.9	18.2	8.7	1,675,905

SOURCE: 1973 NDS.

TABLE 18

Age Distribution by Sex for Intersectoral Migrants, Birth-1965
(percent distribution)

Type of Stream	15-24	25-34	35-49	50+	Total (100 pct.)
			Both Sexes		
Rural-Rural	17.5	21.6	36.6	24.3	1,583,682
Rural-Urban	19.3	21.6	33.8	25.3	1,453,005
Rural-Manila	17.1	24.3	31.4	27.2	661,358
Urban-Urban	22.4	19.1	37.3	21.2	297,279
Urban-Manila	32.0	21.6	27.9	18.5	323,198
Urban-Rural	16.1	22.9	32.1	28.9	461,997
Manila-Rural	39.6	15.3	24.6	20.5	83,127
All	19.5	21.8	33.9	24.8	4,863,646
			Males		
Rural-Rural	17.2	20.7	34.5	27.7	830,911
Rural-Urban	17.3	22.6	32.4	27.6	686,292
Rural-Manila	16.6	21.1	30.9	31.3	323,328
Urban-Urban	21.2	19.5	41.3	18.1	124,633
Urban-Manila	34.0	19.1	28.5	18.4	147,177
Urban-Rural	17.5	19.0	32.2	31.4	223,330
Manila-Rural	38.5	10.3	30.0	21.2	40,579
All	18.8	20.8	33.1	27.3	2,376,250
			Females		
Rural-Rural	17.8	22.7	39.0	20.5	752,771
Rural-Urban	21.1	20.7	35.0	23.2	766,713
Rural-Manila	17.6	27.3	31.9	23.2	338,030
Urban-Urban	23.2	18.8	34.5	23.4	172,646
Urban-Manila	30.3	23.7	27.4	18.5	176,021
Urban-Rural	14.9	26.5	32.1	26.5	238,667
Manila-Rural	40.6	20.0	19.5	19.8	42,548
All	20.2	22.8	34.7	22.3	2,487,396

SOURCE: 1973 NDS.

TABLE 19

Age Distribution by Sex for Nonmigrants, 1973
(percent distribution)

Type of Locale	15-24	25-34	35-49	50+	Total (100 pct.)
			Both Sexes		
Rural	37.9	19.9	23.7	18.5	10,245,334
Urban	42.7	19.8	21.6	15.9	3,177,330
Metropolitan	48.9	20.1	17.4	13.6	928,091
All	39.7	19.9	22.8	17.6	14,350,755
			Males		
Rural	39.0	19.2	22.4	19.3	5,100,621
Urban	45.1	18.7	21.6	14.6	1,556,250
Metropolitan	51.5	20.0	16.6	11.9	458,276
All	41.2	19.2	21.9	17.8	7,115,147
			Females		
Rural	36.8	20.5	24.9	17.8	5,144,713
Urban	40.5	20.9	21.6	17.1	1,621,080
Metropolitan	46.4	20.1	18.1	15.4	469,815
All	38.3	20.6	23.7	17.5	7,235,608

SOURCE: 1973 NDS.

TABLE 20

Sex Ratios for Intersectoral Migrants, 1965-1973, Birth-1965, and Nonmigrants, by Age
(males per 1,000 females)

Type of Stream	15-24	25-34	35-49	50+	Total
			1965-1973 Migrants		
Rural-Rural	91.3	118.7	87.8	130.4	100.8
Rural-Urban	45.2	79.7	94.1	117.2	67.1
Rural-Manila	58.1	70.7	63.7	57.3	60.9
Urban-Urban	51.7	94.7	117.3	132.9	84.2
Urban-Manila	65.0	82.3	91.4	94.0	78.1
Urban-Rural	61.8	98.2	134.1	92.3	90.1
Manila-Rural	79.5	86.6	146.0	140.5	91.7
All	61.1	89.6	96.6	105.6	78.8
			Birth-1965 Migrants		
Rural-Rural	106.7	100.7	97.5	148.8	110.4
Rural-Urban	73.5	98.0	83.1	106.2	89.5
Rural-Manila	90.3	73.9	92.8	129.2	95.7
Urban-Urban	65.8	74.8	86.3	55.7	72.2
Urban-Manila	93.8	67.2	86.9	83.0	83.6
Urban-Rural	110.0	66.9	93.9	110.7	93.6
Manila-Rural	90.5	49.3	146.2	101.8	95.4
All	89.1	87.1	91.2	116.7	95.5
			Nonmigrants		
Type of Locale					
Rural	105.2	93.0	89.4	107.5	99.1
Urban	107.0	86.1	95.9	82.3	96.0
Metropolitan	108.3	97.1	89.4	75.2	97.5
All	105.8	91.7	90.7	100.2	98.3

SOURCE: 1973 NDS.

TABLE 21

Education: Intersectoral Migrants, 1965-1973, by Sex
(percent distribution)

Type of Stream	None	Elementary 1-4	Elementary 5-7	High School Vocational	College or Over	No Information	Total (100 pct.)
Both Sexes							
Rural-Rural	7.0	34.9	34.6	17.6	4.7	1.1	590,594
Rural-Urban	6.6	13.5	28.2	31.0	20.7	0.1	770,988
Rural-Manila	1.2	8.8	29.8	35.1	24.5	0.6	405,361
Urban-Urban	3.1	7.1	22.6	34.9	31.9	0.4	256,196
Urban-Manila	1.1	4.9	21.8	35.0	36.5	0.6	500,068
Urban-Rural	12.9	23.1	24.6	26.9	11.6	0.9	335,093
Manila-Rural	2.6	17.3	35.8	29.7	14.4	0.2	138,518
All	5.2	16.4	28.1	29.4	20.3	0.6	2,996,818
Males							
Rural-Rural	7.1	37.0	34.4	17.0	3.4	1.1	296,503
Rural-Urban	5.9	16.5	24.3	34.2	18.8	0.2	309,474
Rural-Manila	0.9	6.7	19.8	38.6	33.0	1.0	153,449
Urban-Urban	1.8	5.9	23.3	24.5	43.8	0.8	117,120
Urban-Manila	0.7	3.9	17.0	35.5	42.0	1.0	219,253
Urban-Rural	15.5	21.9	18.3	32.0	11.6	0.7	158,845
Manila-Rural	3.2	18.9	30.2	29.5	17.9	0.4	66,269
All	5.4	17.7	24.3	29.7	22.2	0.8	1,320,913

				Females			
Rural-Rural	7.0	32.9	34.7	18.4	6.0	1.1	294,091
Rural-Urban	7.0	11.4	30.8	28.8	21.9	0.1	461,514
Rural-Manila	1.4	10.1	35.9	33.0	19.3	0.3	251,912
Urban-Urban	4.1	8.2	22.0	43.7	22.0	0.0	139,076
Urban-Manila	1.4	5.8	25.6	34.6	32.2	0.4	280,815
Urban-Rural	10.5	24.2	30.3	22.3	11.6	1.0	176,248
Manila-Rural	2.1	15.9	40.9	29.9	11.2	0.0	72,249
All	5.1	15.3	31.0	29.2	18.9	0.4	1,675,905

SOURCE: 1973 NDS.

TABLE 22

Education: Intersectoral Migrants, Birth-1965, by Sex
(percent distribution)

Type of Stream	None	Elementary 1-4	Elementary 5-7	High School Vocational	College or Over	No Information	Total (100 pct.)
Both Sexes							
Rural-Rural	14.4	35.7	29.9	14.3	5.2	0.4	1,583,682
Rural-Urban	7.6	20.4	26.9	26.1	18.3	0.9	1,453,005
Rural-Manila	4.7	11.7	23.8	31.5	27.4	0.9	661,358
Urban-Urban	5.1	15.0	20.1	31.5	28.2	0.1	297,279
Urban-Manila	1.3	10.7	18.7	35.1	32.9	1.2	323,198
Urban-Rural	12.5	36.5	28.8	17.5	4.0	0.6	461,997
Manila-Rural	2.9	15.4	25.6	39.6	16.4	0.0	83,127
All	9.2	24.7	26.6	23.3	15.5	0.7	4,863,646
Males							
Rural-Rural	13.3	35.6	30.3	15.0	5.5	0.3	830,911
Rural-Urban	6.5	19.4	25.2	27.0	21.2	0.7	686,292
Rural-Manila	2.8	9.4	21.3	33.3	32.3	0.9	323,328
Urban-Urban	4.2	13.3	17.4	35.8	29.1	0.2	124,633
Urban-Manila	1.1	6.4	13.2	40.3	37.6	1.4	147,177
Urban-Rural	12.2	37.9	24.5	19.1	5.0	1.3	223,330
Manila-Rural	2.3	8.9	43.6	37.0	8.2	0.0	40,579
All	8.4	24.2	25.5	24.4	16.9	0.7	2,376,250

				Females			
Rural-Rural	15.7	35.8	29.5	13.5	4.9	0.6	752,771
Rural-Urban	8.5	21.3	28.4	25.2	15.6	1.0	766,713
Rural-Manila	6.4	13.9	26.1	29.9	22.8	0.9	338,030
Urban-Urban	5.7	16.2	22.1	28.4	27.6	0.0	172,646
Urban-Manila	1.5	14.2	23.4	30.8	29.1	1.0	176,021
Urban-Rural	12.8	35.2	32.9	16.1	3.1	0.0	238,667
Manila-Rural	3.5	21.7	8.5	42.1	24.3	0.0	42,548
All	10.1	25.2	27.7	22.3	14.1	0.7	2,487,396

SOURCE: 1973 NDS.

TABLE 23

Education: Nonmigrants by Type of Locale, 1973, by Sex
(percent distribution)

Type of Locale	None	Elementary 1-4	Elementary 5-7	High School Vocational	College or Over	No Information	Total (100 pct.)
Both Sexes							
Rural	13.1	28.6	32.2	18.8	6.3	0.9	10,277,402
Urban	6.8	17.1	23.4	30.2	21.2	1.3	3,177,330
Metropolitan	2.9	6.3	15.5	42.4	32.0	0.9	896,023
All	11.1	24.7	29.2	22.8	11.2	1.0	14,350,755
Males							
Rural	11.7	28.5	32.4	21.2	5.3	0.9	5,117,540
Urban	5.4	17.3	22.7	33.3	20.3	1.1	1,556,250
Metropolitan	2.3	4.2	15.3	45.5	31.5	1.2	441,357
All	9.7	24.6	29.2	25.4	10.2	0.9	7,115,147
Females							
Rural	14.5	28.8	32.0	16.6	7.2	0.9	5,159,862
Urban	8.1	16.8	24.0	27.3	22.1	1.6	1,621,080
Metropolitan	3.5	8.3	15.8	39.3	32.4	0.6	454,666
All	12.4	24.8	29.2	20.4	12.1	1.1	7,235,608

SOURCE: 1973 NDS.

TABLE 24

Cash Income: Intersectoral Migrants, 1965-1973, by Sex
(percent distribution)

Type of Stream	<1,000	1,000-2,999	3,000-4,999	5,000+	No Information	Total (100 pct.)
Both Sexes						
Rural-Rural	80.5	11.4	4.6	0.7	2.7	539,051
Rural-Urban	65.0	19.4	8.1	2.7	4.9	681,517
Rural-Manila	66.8	16.1	7.6	5.0	4.5	345,358
Urban-Urban	56.4	19.6	9.4	7.7	6.8	229,600
Urban-Manila	50.9	18.8	14.0	13.1	3.2	431,398
Urban-Rural	71.9	16.3	6.8	3.2	1.7	308,629
Manila-Rural	63.8	13.3	11.7	4.8	6.5	125,152
All	66.1	16.6	8.4	4.9	4.0	2,660,705
Males						
Rural-Rural	68.5	19.7	7.1	1.4	3.3	283,414
Rural-Urban	38.6	40.0	8.3	5.7	7.5	286,122
Rural-Manila	44.5	29.8	12.7	8.3	4.7	130,017
Urban-Urban	34.3	27.6	16.1	14.9	7.1	107,242
Urban-Manila	24.0	28.4	20.3	23.9	3.4	189,229
Urban-Rural	53.9	27.5	10.4	5.0	3.1	154,550
Manila-Rural	44.9	23.3	13.7	9.8	8.3	62,061
All	45.8	28.8	11.6	8.7	5.0	1,212,635

TABLE 24 (cont.)

Type of Stream	<1,000	1,000-2,999	3,000-4,999	5,000+	No Information	Total (100 pct.)
			Females			
Rural-Rural	93.8	2.3	1.8	0.0	2.1	255,637
Rural-Urban	84.1	4.5	7.9	0.5	3.0	395,395
Rural-Manila	80.3	7.9	4.5	3.0	4.4	215,341
Urban-Urban	75.7	12.6	3.6	1.4	6.6	122,358
Urban-Manila	72.0	11.2	9.1	4.6	3.1	242,169
Urban-Rural	90.0	5.1	3.1	1.4	0.4	154,079
Manila-Rural	82.3	3.4	9.6	0.0	4.6	63,091
All	83.1	6.4	5.7	1.6	3.1	1,448,070

SOURCE: 1973 NDS.

TABLE 25

Cash Income: Intersectoral Migrants, Birth-1965, by Sex
(percent distribution)

Type of Stream	<1,000	1,000-2,999	3,000-4,999	5,000+	No Information	Total (100 pct.)
			Both Sexes			
Rural-Rural	71.2	19.7	5.7	1.5	1.9	1,487,437
Rural-Urban	56.8	24.7	10.6	5.8	2.0	1,302,490
Rural-Manila	42.3	22.1	16.3	16.5	2.9	592,619
Urban-Urban	58.1	17.7	15.3	7.5	1.5	265,234
Urban-Manila	49.8	21.4	11.2	13.7	4.0	270,556
Urban-Rural	76.7	16.6	3.4	0.8	2.4	429,074
Manila-Rural	63.6	18.3	8.2	3.2	6.7	70,759
All	61.4	21.2	9.3	5.8	2.3	4,418,169
			Males			
Rural-Rural	54.6	31.7	8.3	2.5	2.9	807,294
Rural-Urban	32.3	39.8	15.4	10.1	2.4	618,458
Rural-Manila	13.5	31.8	24.1	28.2	2.3	290,964
Urban-Urban	37.0	31.9	16.4	13.8	0.8	112,095
Urban-Manila	26.6	29.3	16.6	22.9	4.7	126,477
Urban-Rural	60.8	29.5	4.3	1.6	3.8	207,590
Manila-Rural	51.6	23.8	10.2	6.2	8.3	37,134
All	40.9	33.5	12.9	9.8	2.9	2,200,012

TABLE 25 (cont.)

Type of Stream	<1,000	1,000-2,999	3,000-4,999	5,000+	No Information	Total (100 pct.)
			Females			
Rural-Rural	90.8	5.4	2.7	0.2	0.8	680,143
Rural-Urban	79.0	11.1	6.3	1.9	1.6	684,032
Rural-Manila	70.1	12.6	8.7	5.2	3.4	301,655
Urban-Urban	73.5	7.2	14.5	2.8	1.9	153,139
Urban-Manila	70.1	14.5	6.5	5.6	3.4	144,079
Urban-Rural	91.7	4.6	2.6	0.0	1.1	221,484
Manila-Rural	76.9	12.2	6.1	0.0	4.9	33,625
All	81.7	8.9	5.7	1.9	1.7	2,218,157

SOURCE: 1973 NDS.

TABLE 26

Cash Income: Nonmigrants by Type of Locale, 1973, by Sex
(percent distribution)

Type of Locale	<1,000	1,000-2,999	3,000-4,999	5,000+	No Information	Total (100 pct.)
			Both Sexes			
Rural	75.9	15.5	3.8	1.3	3.4	8,817,803
Urban	63.4	21.2	8.3	3.2	3.8	2,639,741
Metropolitan	55.0	19.4	13.0	7.9	4.7	727,727
All	72.0	17.0	5.4	2.1	3.6	12,185,271
			Males			
Rural	62.7	25.6	4.9	2.0	4.8	4,588,083
Urban	49.1	32.0	8.7	5.2	5.1	1,319,496
Metropolitan	42.9	25.9	15.1	11.5	4.7	367,178
All	58.7	26.9	6.3	3.3	4.8	6,274,757
			Females			
Rural	90.3	4.6	2.6	0.5	1.9	4,229,720
Urban	77.8	10.4	8.0	1.3	2.5	1,320,245
Metropolitan	67.3	12.8	11.0	4.2	4.7	360,549
All	86.1	6.4	4.3	0.9	2.2	5,910,514

SOURCE: 1973 NDS.

BIBLIOGRAPHY

Abelarde, Pedro. 1947. *American Tariff Policy Towards the Philippines.* New York: King's Crown Press.

Abenoja, Macrina. 1975. "Urbanization in the Central and Eastern Visayas." M.A. Thesis, University of the Philippines Population Institute.

Acosta, M., and Hardoy, J. E. 1972. "Urbanization Policies in Revolutionary Cuba." In Geisse, G., and Hardoy, J. E. (eds.), *Latin American Urban Research,* Vol. II. Beverly Hills: Sage Publications. Pp. 167-178.

Agoncillo, Teodoro. 1971. *History of the Filipino People.* Quezon City: RP Garcia Publishing Company.

Arriaga, Eduardo E. 1968. "Components of City Growth in Selected Latin American Countries." *Milbank Memorial Fund Quarterly* 46:237-252.

Artle, Roland. 1970. "Urbanization and Economic Growth in Venezuela." Reprint No. 73. Berkeley: University of California, Institute of Urban and Regional Development.

Bennett, Don C. 1965. "The New Official Definition of the Urban Population in the Philippines: A Critique." *The Philippine Geographic Journal* 9 (January-June).

Brutzkus, Eliezer. 1975. "Centralized Versus Decentralized Pattern of Urbanization in Developing Countries: An Attempt to Elucidate a Guideline Principle." *Economic Development and Cultural Change* 23 (July): 633-652.

Carvajal, Manuel V., and Geithman, David T. 1974. "An Economic Analysis of Migration in Costa Rica." *Economic Development and Cultural Change* 23 (October): 105-122.

Concepcion, Mercedes B. 1974. "Changes in Period Fertility as Gleaned from the 1973 NDS." Research Note No. 13. University of the Philippines Population Institute (mimeo).

Cressey, Paul F. 1958. "The Development of Philippine Cities." *Silliman Journal* 5.

_____. 1960. "Urbanization in the Philippines." *Sociology and Social Research* 44 (July): 402-409.

Davis, Kingsley. 1965. "The Urbanization of the Human Population." *Scientific American* 213:40-53.

_____. 1969. *"World Urbanization 1950-1970, Vol. I: Basic Data for Cities, Countries, and Regions.* Berkeley: University of California, Institute of International Studies.

_____. 1972. *World Urbanization 1950-1970. Vol. II: Analysis of Trends, Relation-*

ships, and Development. Berkeley: University of California, Institute of International Studies.

Domingo, Lita, and Zosa, Imelda. 1975. "Regional Trends in Activity, Employment Status, and Industry." Research Note No. 73. University of the Philippines Population Institute (mimeo).

Dotson, Arch, and Teune, Henry. 1972. "Urbanization and National Development: A Probable Case." Paper for the SEADAG Seminar on Urbanization and National Development Planning, Manila (January 4-7).

Dovring, F. 1959. "The Share of Agriculture in a Growing Population." *Monthly Bulletin of Agricultural Economics and Statistics* 8. Rome: FAO (August-September).

Duncan, Otis D., et al. 1961. *Statistical Geography: Problems in Analyzing Areal Data.* Glencoe, Ill.: Free Press.

Durand, John D., and Pelaez, Cesar A. 1965. "Patterns of Urbanization in Latin America." *Milbank Memorial Fund Quarterly* 43:166-191.

Eldridge, Hope Tisdale. 1942. "The Process of Urbanization." *Social Forces* 20 (March).

Esmundo, Rafael. 1975. "Total Integrated Development Approach: A Human Response." *Population Forum,* Monthly Newsletter of the Commission on Population (November).

Feitosa, Lucia Maria. 1975. "Internal Migration in the Philippines: A Study on Migration Differentials." Ph.D. Dissertation. Department of Sociology, Brown University.

Friedmann, John. 1968. "The Strategy of Deliberate Urbanization." *American Institute of Planners Journal* 34:364-373.

Fuguitt, Glenn V., and Zuiches, James J. 1975. "Residential Preferences and Population Distribution." *Demography* 12 (August): 491-504.

Fujimoto, Isao. 1968. "The Social Complexity of Philippine Towns and Cities." *Solidarity* 3 (May): 76-90.

Fuller, Gary, and Chapman, Murray. 1974. "On the Role of Mental Maps in Migration Research." *International Migration Review* 8 (Winter): 491-506.

Gottman, Jean. 1961. *Megalopolis: The Urbanized Northeastern Seaboard of the United States.* New York: The Twentieth Century Fund.

Grebenik, E., and Leridon, H. 1973. "Demographic Research Needed." IUSSP Papers No. 1. Liege, Belgium.

Greenwood, Michael J. 1975. "Simultaneity Bias in Migration Models: An Empirical Examination." *Demography* 12 (August): 519-536.

Hart, Donn V. 1971. "Philippine Rural-Urban Migration: A View from Caticugan, a Bisayan Village." *Behavioral Science Notes* 6:103-137.

Hendershot, Gerry E. 1969. "Challenge to Urbanization in the Seventies." In Concepcion, M. B. (ed.), *Philippine Population in the Seventies.* Manila: Community Publishers, Inc.

_____. 1971. "Cityward Migration and Urban Fertility in the Philippines." *Philippine Sociological Review* 19:183-191.

Hicks, George L., and McNicoll, Geoffrey. 1971. *Trade and Growth in the Philippines.* Ithaca: Cornell University Press.

Hollnsteiner, Mary R. 1969. "The Urbanization of Metropolitan Manila." In Bello, Walden F., and de Guzman, Alfonso, II (eds.), *Modernization: Its Impact in the Philippines IV.* Quezon City: Ateneo de Manila University Press.

_____. 1974. "Urban Planning: A Curbside View." *Philippine Planning Journal* 5 (April): 65-72.

Hoselitz, Bert F. 1953. "The Role of Cities in the Economic Growth of Underdeveloped Countries." *Journal of Political Economy* 61:195-208.

International Bank for Reconstruction and Development. 1972. *World Bank Atlas.* Washington, D.C.

International Labour Office. 1959 and 1972. *Yearbook of Labour Statistics.* Geneva.

_____. 1974. *Sharing in Development: A Programme of Employment, Equity, and Growth for the Philippines.* Geneva.

Jacobson, Leo, and Prakash, Ved. 1968. "Urbanization and Regional Planning in India." *Ekistics* (March): 158-165.

Jefferson, Mark. 1939. "The Law of the Primate City." *Geographical Review* 29 (April): 226-232.

Johnston, J. 1963. *Econometric Methods.* 2d Ed. New York: McGraw-Hill.

Jones, Gavin. 1972. "Implications of Prospective Urbanization for Development Planning in Southeast Asia." Paper presented at the SEADAG Population Panel Seminar on the Urban Focus, Pattaya, Thailand (June 11-14).

Keyfitz, Nathan. 1972. "Population Theory and Doctrine: A Historical Survey." In Petersen, William (ed.), *Readings in Population.* New York: The Macmillan Company. Pp. 41-69.

Kim, Yun. 1972. "Net Internal Migration in the Philippines, 1960-1970." *Journal of Philippine Statistics* 23 (July): 9-29.

Kindleberger, Charles P. 1958. *Economic Development.* New York: McGraw-Hill.

Kumar, Joginder. 1973. *Population and Land in World Agriculture: Recent Trends and Relationships.* Berkeley: University of California, Institute of International Studies.

Lampard, Eric E. 1955. "The History of Cities in Economically Advanced Areas." In Friedmann, John, and Alonso, William (eds.), *Regional Development and Planning.* Cambridge: MIT Press, 1964.

Laquian, Aprodicio A. 1966. *The City in Nation-Building.* Manila: University of the Philippines, School of Public Administration.

Lerner, Daniel. 1967. "Comparative Analysis of Processes of Modernization." In Miner, Horace (ed.), *The City in Modern Africa.* New York: Praeger.

Lewis, Robert A., et al. 1974. "Urbanization and Urban Policy in USSR: 1959-1970." Paper presented at the Annual Meeting of the Population Association of America, New York City (April).

Mangahas, Mahar. 1975. "The Measurement of Philippine National Welfare." Social Indicators Project. Development Academy of the Philippines.

Marcos, Ferdinand. 1972. "Presidential Decree No. 79: Revising the Population Act of 1971." Manila.

Mariano, Vicente. 1975. "Urbanization and Internal Migration in Forty-Five Philippine Cities in the 1960s." M.A. Thesis, University of the Philippines Population Institute.

McGee, T. G. 1967. *The Southeast Asian City: A Social Geography of the Primate Cities of Southeast Asia.* London: G. Bell and Sons.

———. 1971. *The Urbanization Process in the Third World.* London: G. Bell and Sons, Ltd.

Murphey, Rhoads. 1966. "Urbanization in Asia." *Ekistics* 21 (January): 8-17.

Myint, Hla. 1972. *Southeast Asia's Economy: Development Policies in the 1970s.* New York: Praeger.

Myrdal, Gunnar. 1968. *Asian Drama: An Inquiry into the Poverty of Nations.* New York: Pantheon Press.

National Census and Statistics Office. 1972a. "Urban Population of the Philippines by Category, Region, Province, City and Municipality: 1970." Special Report No. 2.

———. 1972b. "Population, Land Area, Density and Per cent Change in Three Censal Years, 1948, 1960 and 1970: Philippines." Special Report No. 3.

———. 1972c. "Income and Expenditures in the Philippines: 1971." (An Economic Situation Report). Special Release No. 139-A.

———. 1973. "The Growth of Urban Population in the Philippines and Its Perspectives." Technical Paper No. 5.

Nava, E. L. 1959. "Internal Migration in the Philippines, 1939-1948." Paper presented to the Demographic Training and Research Centre, Bombay, India.

Nazaret, Francisco V., and Barretto, Felisa R. 1963. "Concepts and Definitions of Urban-Rural Areas in the Philippines." *The Philippine Statistician* 12 (June-September): 89-108.

Nelson, Joan M. 1969. "Migrants, Urban Poverty, and Instability in Developing Nations." Occasional Papers in International Affairs, No. 22. Cambridge: Harvard University Center for International Affairs.

Pascual, Elvira M. 1966. "Population Distribution in the Philippines." Manila: Population Institute, University of the Philippines.

———. 1972. "Urbanization in the Philippines." Paper presented at the SEADAG Population Panel Seminar on the Urban Focus, Pattaya, Thailand (June 11-14).

Phelan, J. L. 1959. *The Hispanization of the Philippines: Spanish Aims and Filipino Responses, 1565-1700.* Madison, Wis.: University of Wisconsin Press.

Reed, Robert R. 1967. "Hispanic Urbanism in the Philippines: A Study of the Impact of Church and State." *Journal of East Asiatic Studies,* University of Manila, 2 (March).

———. 1972. "The Primate City in Southeast Asia: Conceptual Definitions and Colonial Origins." *Asian Studies* 10 (December): 283-320.

Republic of the Philippines. 1973. *Four-Year Development Plan, FY 1974-77.* Manila: National Economic and Development Authority.

Schnore, Leo F. 1961. "The Statistical Measurement of Urbanization and Economic Development." *Land Economics* 37:229-245.

Sicat, Gerardo. 1972. *Economic Policy and Philippine Development.* Quezon City: University of the Philippines Press.

Simkins, Paul D., and Wernstedt, Frederick L. 1963. "Growth and Internal Migrations of the Philippine Population, 1948-1960." *Journal of Tropical Geography* 17 (May): 197-203.

———. 1971. *Philippine Migration: The Settlement of the Digos-Padada Valley, Davao Province.* Monograph Series No. 16. New Haven: Yale University Southeast Asia Studies.

Smith, Peter C. 1970. "Areal Differentiation and the Urbanization Process in Lowland Luzon." Ph.D. Dissertation, Department of Sociology, University of Chicago.

———. 1974a. "Distribution of Population by Age, Sex, and Marital Status, May 1973: Urban-Rural and Regional Patterns." Research Note No. 19. University of the Philippines Population Institute (mimeo).

———. 1974b. "Identifying Inter-Provincial Migration Streams in the Philippines: An Approach to the Analysis of Destination-Origin Matrices." Paper presented at the Fourth Organization of Demographic Associates Conference, Manila (January 21-25).

———. 1975a. "Interregional Migration: Lifetime and 1960-1970: (1) Magnitudes of the Total Streams and (2) Sex Ratios in the Streams." Research Notes Nos. 69 and 70. University of the Philippines Population Institute (mimeo).

———. 1975b. "Fertility in Metropolitan, Other Urban and Rural Areas: A Decomposition into Sources of Variation, 1968-1972." Research Note No. 40. University of the Philippines Population Institute (mimeo).

———. 1975c. "The Turn-of-the-Century Birth Rate: Estimates from Birth Registration and Age Structure." In Flieger, Wilhelm, and Smith, P. C., *A Demographic Path to Modernity.* Quezon City: University of the Philippines Press.

———, and Bouis, Howarth. 1975. "An Approach to Delimiting Social and Economic Concentrations Through Scalograms: Mindanao, 1972." Research Note No. 41. University of the Philippines Population Institute (mimeo).

———, et al. 1975. "Preliminary Estimates of National-Level Mortality, 1960-1968, and 1973, and Mortality Differentials Around 1970." Research Note No. 43. University of the Philippines Population Institute (mimeo).

Spencer, J. E. 1958. "The Cities of the Philippines." *Journal of Geography* 57.

Terzo, Frederick C. 1972. *Urbanization in the Developing Countries: The Response of International Assistance.* International Urbanization Survey. New York: The Ford Foundation.

Todaro, Michael P. 1969. "A Model of Labor Migration and Urban Unemployment in Less Developed Countries." *American Economic Review* 59 (March): 138-148.

Ulack, Richard. 1972. "The Impact of Industrialization upon the Migration and Demographic Characteristics of Iligan City, Mindanao." Ph.D. Dissertation, Pennsylvania State University.

Ullman, Edward. 1960. "Trade Centers and Tributary Areas of the Philippines." *Geographical Review* 50 (April).

UNESCO. 1957. *Urbanization in Asia and the Far East.* Hauser, Philip M. (ed.). Calcutta: Research Center on the Social Implications of Industrialization in Southeast Asia.

United Nations. 1948 and 1964. *Demographic Yearbook.* New York.

_____. 1970. *Methods of Measuring Internal Migration.* Manual VI, Manuals on Methods of Estimating Population. New York.

_____. 1973a. *Statistical Yearbook, 1972.* New York.

_____. 1973b. *Yearbook of National Accounts Statistics, 1971.* Vol. III. New York.

_____. 1974. *Methods for Projections of Urban and Rural Population.* Manual VIII, Manuals on Methods of Estimating Population. New York.

U.S. Bureau of the Census. 1961. *Historical Statistics of the United States: Colonial Times to 1957.* Washington, D.C.

_____. 1973. *Statistical Abstract of the United States, 1972.* Washington, D.C.

Vandermeer, Canute, and Agaloos B. C. 1961. "Twentieth Century Settlement of Mindanao." Paper No. 47. Michigan Academy of Science, Arts and Letters. Pp. 537-548.

Weber, Adna F. 1899. *The Growth of Cities in the Nineteenth Century: A Study in Statistics.* New York: The Macmillan Company.

Weitz, Raanan (ed.) 1973. *Urbanization and the Developing Countries.* New York: Praeger.

Wonnacott, Ronald J., and Wonnacott, Thomas H. 1970. *Econometrics.* New York: John Wiley and Sons.

Worcester, Dean C. 1914. *The Philippines: Past and Present.* New York: The Macmillan Company.

Woytinsky, W. S., and Woytinsky, E. S. 1950. *World Population and Production: Trends and Outlook.* New York: The Twentieth Century Fund.

Yoder, Michael L., and Fuguitt, Glenn V. 1974. "Urbanization, Frontier Growth, and Population Redistribution in Brazil, 1960-1970." Revision of a Paper presented at the Annual Meeting of the Population Association of America, New York City (April).

Zablan, Zelda C. 1975. "Regional Differentials in Mortality: Philippines, 1973." Research Note No. 64. University of the Philippines Population Institute (mimeo).

Zachariah, K. C., and Pernia, E. M. 1975. "Migration in the Philippines with Particular Reference to Less Developed Regions." Report prepared for the World Bank.

Zosa, Imelda A. 1973. "An Exploratory Survey on the Determinants of Interprovincial Migration." M.A. Thesis, University of the Philippines Population Institute.

INDEX

ABOUT THE AUTHOR

Ernesto M. Pernia, assistant professor at the School of Economics, University of the Philippines, Quezon City, specializes in population and human resources.